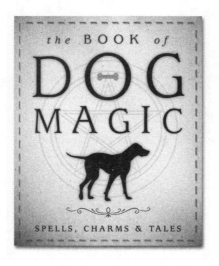

the BOOK of

DOG
MAGIC

SPELLS, CHARMS & TALES

Disclaimer

The publisher and the author assume no liability for any injuries caused to the reader or the reader's pet that may result from the reader's use of content contained in this publication. We recommend common sense when contemplating the practices described in this work.

the BOOK of
DOG
MAGIC

SPELLS, CHARMS & TALES

SOPHIA
with Denny Sargent

Llewellyn Publications
Woodbury, Minnesota

FIRST EDITION
First Printing, 2016

Book design: Donna Burch-Brown
Cover design: Kevin R. Brown
Cover art: iStockphoto.com/9177498/©Michael Henderson
    iStockphoto.com/14009459/©rangepuppies
    iStockphoto.com/38834602/©moggara12
    iStockphoto.com/23933332/©edge69
Interior art credits: Chapters 1, 4, 8, 9, and 10: iStockphoto.com/37468386/
    HelgaMariah
    Chapters 2, 3, and 6: iStockphoto.com/19439047/HelgaMariah
    Chapters 5: iStockphoto.com/53927456/RobinOlimb
    Chapter 7: iStockphoto.com/14009459/rangepuppies

Llewellyn Publications is a registered trademark of Llewellyn Worldwide Ltd.

Library of Congress Cataloging-in-Publication Data

Names: Sophia, 1955–
Title: The book of dog magic : spells, charms & tales / by Sophia, with Denny Sargent.
Description: First Edition. | Woodbury : Llewellyn Worldwide, Ltd, 2016. | Includes bibliographical references.
Identifiers: LCCN 2015037459 | ISBN 9780738746388
Subjects: LCSH: Human-animal communication--Miscellanea. | Dogs--Miscellanea. | Magic. | Astrology. | Chakras.
Classification: LCC BF1623.A55 S67 2016 | DDC 133/.2599772--dc23 LC record available at http://lccn.loc.gov/2015037459

Llewellyn Publications
A Division of Llewellyn Worldwide Ltd.
2143 Wooddale Drive
Woodbury, MN 55125-2989
www.llewellyn.com

Printed in the United States of America

To Our Noble Magical Dog Thor
For 17 years he guarded, guided, helped,
healed, and loved our family with all
his heart and soul. May we all strive to be like him.

And to that little bit of werewolf in each of us...

© Joan Poor

About the Authors

Sophia

Sophia's grandparents taught her how to be a psychic and use her intuitive powers in a number of ways. Through them, Sophia mastered many kinds of divination, such as playing card readings, crystal ball readings, and tea leaf and coffee ground readings to name a few. Also her grandparents trained her in the art of being a medium. She regularly teaches workshops and classes on many of these subjects and gives professional readings.

Sophia is a popular, best-selling New Age author and ceramic artist. She is also an animal intuitive and worldwide traveler. She has the ability to call wild animals to her whereever she goes.

Sophia's web site: www.psychicsophia.com

On Facebook as: Psychic Sophia

Denny Sargent

Denny is a writer, artist, and university instructor who was first introduced to mythology and magick in New York, where he grew up. Ancient cultures and folklore became a lifelong obsession and have informed all his writing. He has an MA in History/Cross Cultural Communications from Western Washington University, where he also taught. He has been initiated into a number of esoteric, Western Hermetic, and Tantrika traditions. He has helped found, write, and edit several esoteric journals of contemporary mythology and magick, such as *Mandragore, Kalika, Aeon,* and *Silverstar.*

Denny lived in Japan and continues to engage in extensive traveling research around the globe. Everywhere, there are dogs. His previously published books include *Global Ritualism, The Tao of Birth Days, The Magical Garden* (co-written with Sophia), *Your Guardian Angel and You, Clean Sweep,* and *Dancing with Spirits.* He loves all animals, especially canines, and has been known to mysteriously disappear during the full moon.

On Facebook as: Denny Sargent

Acknowledgments

We would like to acknowledge the help of Peter Carr, editor-proofreader and amazing pal, and to our friends who gave suggestions and encouraged this work. Thanks and deep gratitude to the great dog gurus in our past and present: Fido, Hugo, Rufus, Pup, Pepe, Pepe Boru, Petey, Kilo, Rex, Beetles DeBop, Kamala, Rachel, Gris John, Tara, Buddy (both of them), Dylan, Bacon, and Tux. Also, to our new puppy, Wolf! Thanks to all the other awesome dogs and dog people we know and love. OM.

Contents

Spells, Charms & Meditations

Chapter Ten

Chapter One

The Magical Dog & Dog Spells

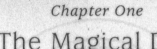

An Introduction

How important are dogs in our lives?

Well, in our house, our dog has been the glue that holds the home and each of us together in so many ways. He is the one that loves you when you come home upset and depressed after a terrible workday and makes you feel instantly better. He is the one that gives love and comfort and help whenever needed, without asking for anything in return. Okay, maybe he'll request (insistently) some doggie treats and a hug or two.

If you have a dog, you know what I mean. The bond we have with our furry familiars is deep and far-reaching. A day doesn't go by without reading an article about some dog saving a child or a dog helping someone with special needs. We spend hours watching cute puppies on YouTube because it makes us feel good.

Dogs, simply said, make us happy. They also do many other things for us because they love us and we love them. Our dog, Thor, not only loved and made us howl with laughter but he also protected us, guided us, helped us find our son when he got lost, warned us of dangers, chased away vermin, and provided healing and love when we needed it most. Dogs always give us unconditional love. No matter how they are treated, dogs almost always respond with devotion. What an awesome being to do so much for so little.

We Love Our Dogs

We have traveled to dozens of countries together, and everywhere we went we saw dogs doing what they have done for thousands of years—everything I've mentioned and more. Our relationship with our amazing dog and our doggish encounters all over the world led us to seriously consider the powerful and important relationship we, as people, have with our dogs.

As we researched, we were astounded to find the same myths, stories, ideas, and symbols as well as both practical and magical connections between our two species reflected in most every culture. The traditional and current benefits and aspects that magical dogs bring to our world are embodied in myth, magic, religion, and shared cultural wisdom.

Dogs are a subset of what are called canines. The term *canine* (originally meaning "pointed tooth") comes from the Latin *caninus*. Eventually, it was used interchangeably with "dog." In this book, we consider all canines dogs.

How did dogs become part of our lives to such an extent? The current theory is that some 40,000 years ago some of the wolves that followed human tribes began to change their relationship with these strange bipedal beings. This symbiotic relationship between canines and primitive humans has evolved and grown in the tens of thousands of years that followed. Canines are both carnivores and scavengers, and it is likely wolves and other canines followed primitive human tribes—first as predators, but over time because they could scavenge food scraps left behind. Their fear and mistrust of people shifted toward a view of us being a constant source of food, thus helping them survive.

It is likely these wild canines began getting closer to the fires of the tribes to get warmth and food. As people began to make friends with them, these wild dogs became a great help in tracking game and emerged as the watchdogs of the tribe, alerting tribal members to potential danger. Archaeological evidence shows that domesticated canines fought off wild wolves, bears, and other threatening creatures. As the relationship developed, humans learned to breed dogs to bring out the most desirable domesticated qualities. Eventually wolves evolved into dogs that became more than wary friends; they became family.

Evidence shows dogs helped ancient man hunt from the earliest days, and their ability to find animals by tracking was likely seen as magical and divine. Dogs are depicted in cave paintings as helping to bring down huge game and also as companions. Some argue that we might literally owe our survival as a species to the help that dogs provided as we were struggling with hunger, disease, lack of fur and fang, ice ages, and an altogether inhospitable world. It must have been wonderful discovering an ally, and things remain the same today.

We experienced this primitive interconnection between people and canines when we traveled the western desert of Egypt and camped with Bedouins. At night, we saw the glowing eyes of the fennecs, small foxlike canines, waiting patiently for the scraps of our meals, which our Bedouin guide took out and left in the dunes. He informed us that this relationship existed as far back as his tribe could remember. In turn, the fennecs watched out for the few harmful creatures that might be about, such as snakes.

Magical Dogs Around the World

Every news day brings a story of a dog rescuing a family or finding a survivor in rubble or whose steadfast protection saves a small child. As companions or service animals, they help people with PTSD, dementia, diabetes, autism, depression, anxiety, and a myriad of other issues. Dogs are a source of joy and solace to those who are alone. In our family, the love and support of our dog helped us survive real tragedies and traumas.

Most people recognize that there is something magical about dogs. Over a third of households in the United States now own dogs, and a 2013 article in *Psychology Today* estimated there were 525 million pet dogs in the world at that time. This may make dogs the most popular pet of all.

Dogs are not just beloved members of the family but also serve as work dogs and sometimes act as spiritual as well as physical guardians. Dog spirit is seen this way in Aboriginal culture and the dingo was both totemic ancestor and beloved member of the family in Australian Aboriginal societies.

In many places, dogs are part of the family, unlike most other animals. In Mongolia, dogs are adopted just like children. In Egypt, dogs were mummified and buried, often next to their people, under the auspices of the canine-headed god of the dead, Anubis. Similar practices are common in many ancient and current cultures. One of the most ornate and beautiful places we visited in Japan was a pet cemetery next to a human one. Inside were shrines filled with photos and mementos. A small central Buddhist temple was dedicated to the souls of these beloved pets whose owners often resided next door.

Dogs and healing have been entwined in magical and practical concepts from the dawn of history. The healing power of dogs is now well documented. In our family, whenever we were stressed or sick, our dog was right there to comfort and help heal us. I remember many times when I had the flu or my partner was quite ill and our dog quietly lay with us, maybe he would lick us, but often just be *with* us. He made us feel better, and in a powerful, mystical way actually appeared to help heal us with dog-love energy.

Those of us with dogs are not surprised, but this moves the healing power of dogs into the realm of demonstrable reality when before it used to be part of faith. There are several healing gods and goddesses represented by dogs or who have them as symbols. A dog often represented Aesculapius, the healer god of ancient Greece, whose snake-entwined staff is still a symbol of medicine. Dogs were common at Aesculapius's temples, which were ancient hospitals. A dog symbolized the Sumerian goddess Gula, and her temples were also centers of healing.

Service dogs help people recover from many physical and mental problems. A book called *Paws & Effect: The Healing Power of Dogs* by Sharon Saks contains astounding data that seems almost mystical. For example, one Japanese study cited in this book found pet owners made 30 percent fewer visits to doctors. An Australian study of six thousand people showed that owners of dogs have lower cholesterol, blood pressure, and heart attack risk compared with people who do not have a dog.

It is said in many cultures that when we pass on dog spirits and dog gods guide us through the perils of the afterlife so we can reach paradise or rebirth. Even today in Japan, Iran, and many other places, the idea that dog spirits can help guide us "on the other side" is part of many funerary traditions. I think all of us dog owners, in our hearts, hope to see our faithful dogs waiting for us when we pass on.

We have clearly been letting dogs guide us for thousands of years, in this world and the next. How many dog owners have gotten lost somewhere and had their dogs guide them home or back to a place they knew? We have gotten turned around in a local state park and simply followed our dog back to the entrance.

Things have not changed very much. Long ago, when finding a safe path for the tribe and successful hunting kept starvation at bay, it was dogs that helped to keep us safe and well fed. They guided us, physically and spiritually, and so it is even today.

As a child, I hunted ducks with my father, and it was always a marvel to see the dogs take over once we were in the marsh, mysteriously following an invisible scent right to the prey and then flushing the ducks and pointing to them. Once we were in the fields, it was all up to the dogs. It was obvious as a kid that this was some kind of amazing magic.

As a child, my dog barked at things that we could not see, occasionally chasing unseen "visitors" out of our very old home. Later, as a married grown-up interested in the spiritual world, I noticed that my dog would often appear to see things that I could not see or follow things with his eyes that were not part of my reality. It is claimed dogs see things we can't see, whether they are ghosts or strange energies of some sort. We trust them in this way, though we might not like to admit it. Our dog once showed great agitation for no apparent reason right before we received a phone call about an accident and again, years later, before we learned about the death of a family member. Coincidence? Many dog owners have similar stories.

Even now, if our dog balks at going someplace spooky or odd, we are likely going to pay attention to his superior senses and go where he says to go. What would we do without guidance from our dogs?

No one is more loyal than a dog and watching the news recently, this has been very evident. There was the dog that protected a lost autistic boy from danger. Then there was the story of the terrier that became lost when a family moved and tracked the family across country successfully. Reports of rescue dogs finding victims in a recent Nepalese earthquake and photos of a dog that died with his master rather than flee the Fukushima Tsunami in Japan that trapped many victims are recent stories that come to mind.

It has been said that dogs are the only pets that will readily die for you, and it is common for dogs to pass on shortly after their human companion has died. I recently read a story about an elderly woman passing on after her dog died, so we see that this deep love and devotion goes both ways. Dogs are not just heroes; they are powerful symbols of love and devotion.

Dogs in Folklore & Mythology

Canines are the most referenced animals in mythology, and we know this because we spent over a year researching them. Many other wild animals and pets have divine stories, rituals, and symbolism attached to them, but dogs are so universally loved for their loyalty, healing, and companionship that they occupy a very special place in almost all religions, faiths, and myth cycles all over the world.

Canines protected humanity from the beginning, but they continue protecting us spiritually as tradition and folklore tell us. *Shi*, or Lion-Dogs, are often called *Foo Dogs* or "magic dogs". They have protected temples, homes, and people across Asia for thousands of years. Almost every temple in China has Foo Dog statues out front, driving away evil of all kinds. Paper charms with sacred symbols and Foo Dogs on them are burned in rituals to drive away evil spirits.

The dog-headed god Anubis was an ancient Egyptian guardian of the spirits of the dead and the living. It was a divine golden dog that protected baby Zeus and whose image represented such protection in ancient Greece. In Nordic countries, the runic symbols called "wolf hook" and "eye of the wolf" can still be seen, banishing evil and protecting places and people. For most of human history and even today, dogs and dog magic have protected our homes, our physical bodies, and also our spiritual world.

One reason we got our dog so many years ago was to help protect our home. I'm sure most people getting dogs have the same idea. What surprised us was how deeply and personally our dog took this instinctual duty. When our dog was only a few months old, a stranger approached and this little fur ball jumped in front of my wife and growled a tiny, not very scary growl with every fiber of his little body. Many years later, when a mentally unstable man came to our door with the clear intention of harming us, our normally calm and super-friendly dog transformed into a frightening, snarling, barking wolf in front of me, scaring the hostile thug away. My brother Scott, another dog lover and ex-canine corps officer, once told us that alarms can be rigged but a dog is by far the best security anyone can possess, and I agree. Good dogs!

Philosophers from Plato and Pliny to Saint Augustine viewed dogs as a paramount symbol of spiritual and physical guidance. In myth, a dog (Anubis) even helped guide the sun as it traversed through the Egyptian underworld. In Aztec mythology, it is the dog god Xolotl who does the same thing, guiding the sun through the underworld and thus saving us each day. The Celtic Herne the hunter, the Norse Odin, and or the Welsh Arawn are guided by spirit dogs as they fly through the sky in the "Wild Hunt," a spiritual whirlwind of gods, faerie, and supernatural beings said to fly about signaling the beginning of winter. Artemis hunted with her sacred dogs as did the many other gods and goddesses, and they all relied on their dogs for success.

Mythically dogs represent clan or family love. For millennia canines also represented sexual love in myths and beliefs. When in heat or looking for love, nothing matches the sexual adventurousness of a dog. The ease with which dogs conceive and give birth made them common magical symbols for fertility. In myths, dogs accompany gods and goddesses of fertility such as Diana, Innana, and Pan. "Coyote" spirit has many stories of his sexual adventures still told today among Native American tribes. Even in our most primal emotions, dogs are front and center.

Canines and dogs have also been mythic symbols and magical manifestations of the power of loyalty, devotion, and fidelity since time immemorial. The symbolic image of fidelity drawn in the Middle Ages depicts a female muse with a dog. Similar divine heroes such as Odysseus and King Arthur had mystically inspired divine dogs that epitomized loyalty and devotion. The Hindu gods Bhairav Shiva and Vishnu, the Chinese god Erlang, and the Norse god Odin have canines that accompany them with deep devotion and loyalty.

In India, there is a story of devotion going both ways. The god Indra offered to take the hero Yudhisthira to heaven in his chariot as a reward. When Yudhishtira asked for his dog to join him, Indra refused. Yudhisthira declined to enter heaven without his dog, who had saved him in battle many times. Indra relented and not only did the dog enter heaven, but it was transformed into the god Dharma.

A loyal dog also was said to protect the Buddha, and so dogs are an important symbol in Tibetan Buddhism. Buddhist saints and even monks are said to magically appear as dogs. Some Buddhists refer to dogs as excellent teachers of loyalty and devotion.

Dogs served as mystical guides, as protectors, as "familiars," and as givers of omens for as long as magical things have been noted. Such mythic dog beings, including the Celtic Cu Sith, giant green faerie dogs, or the infamous Black Dog spirit of Scotland and England, foretold dramatic and personal events for centuries.

Dog magic was an important part of the healing magic of the Middle Eastern goddess Belit-ili, the powerful magic of the African god Legba, and of the sorcery of Hecate and Artemis. A canine's breath is said to banish evil, the skin can make spells manifest, and the saliva can heal, or so the old tales tell us. Dogs are themselves considered magic makers and various gods, goddesses, and spirits manifest as dogs. Odin and Legba appear as dogs, and Old Man Coyote of Native American fame will show up as a human or his namesake to trick or to help. Dog spirits act as special otherworldly messengers for Hermes, Hecate, and many others.

Dog talismans are used in sending prayers to the gods, guarding graves, and banishing evil. Siberian shamans rely on their dog spirit for guidance during their out-of-body travels, and special dogs, just by their very presence, act as magical beings and living amulets.

Dogs help those of us who are psychic balance energies, connect with our powers, describe the unseen world, give us good energy, and help with what Native American shamans call "dog medicine." If you work with magic, energies, or the psychic world, it is always a good idea to have positive "dog medicine."

Dogs are our loyal companions, comforters, healers, and friends in life and, according to thousands of years of lore, they continue to guide, help, and protect us even in death. And when we pass on, the ancient Egyptians believed we become stars in the sky. This is where the great Dog Spirit resides, shining forth upon us as Canis Major, whose heart is the "Dog Star" Sirius. Much lore surrounds this great Dog Spirit that, the Greeks tell us, Zeus placed in the heavens for a job well done. The ancient Egyptian year began with the rising of Sopdet (Sirius) also signaling the beginning of the cycle of life and death. Sothis cast its power across the Greek and Roman worlds as well.

Across continents we see myriad other celestial dog myths, including the wild star dog of China, which can emit positive "Yang" powers, or which can manifest baneful energies to cause disasters. In Asia, the animal zodiac heaps praises upon those born in the Year of the Dog, saying they are loyal and giving. The ancient myths mention the star power of dogs in many other ways. No matter how you view it, dogs seem to know they are stars, though they are strongly connected to the moon and the sun. It is safe to say every dog is the star of its own story and this is how we honor and treat them.

Well, now you know a few of the myths and stories about magical dogs, and we have more to tell you, but all the magic is really in how you and your dog live and love and enter the spirit world together. What will help you do that are dog spells.

Dog Spells & You

Dog image charms, canine runes and amulets, and even hair, skin, and teeth from canines were components of spells and rituals in many cultures. The earliest shamans, witches, sorcerers, and magic makers called upon dog spirits, constructed canine talismans, and, of course, possessed their own dog familiars to help in their magic making. And now you can as well.

You will find each section that follows begins with a passage describing folklore, myths, and mystical tidbits to open your mind to what a rich and numinous spiritual history dogs possess. The spells, charms, and meditations in this book are for both the practicing dog-loving magic maker and for the dog lover who has never cast a spell or even thought of dog magic before. Never fear, these spells, charms, and meditations are for everyone!

For those not so familiar with "real" magic, let's chat about spells in general and dog spells in particular. Spells, charms, and meditations are magical practices to accomplish something on a spiritual or energetic level. Often they include ritual actions, simple ingredients, and some special words of power. Spells and charms are traditionally used to cause change in the physical world in accordance with the will of the magic maker by focusing spiritual power.

Do you believe in mind over matter? Do you think prayer or meditation can change aspects of your world? If you do, then this is what spells are. Think of them as guided prayers or spiritual recipes for using energy to make things happen in a positive way on many levels.

Dogs have a long, deep connection to magic and to spiritual practices. There are many gods and goddesses who have been associated with dogs for thousands of years and you will encounter many of them in this book. Most, like Hermes, will be familiar to the reader. Some, however, are more unusual and can all be found in a glossary near the end of this book. Their names are used in the spells in each section to help unlock the mythic and archetypal powers of your inner mind in order to help your dog and you.

Many of the spells also include words of power in a variety of other languages, such as ancient Greek, Sanskrit, and Latin. At the end of each spell, a translation of these phrases can be found.

The various words of power in the spells may seem odd, and the question arises, why use Greek, Sanskrit, or Latin at all when English translations might just as easily suffice? The answer in most cases is to retain the power behind what the words represent in each spell—to help you both understand and intuit the essence behind the concepts presented in the vibrations of the original language.

According to the philosophy of magic, the names of gods, spirits, and sacred forces are bound into the sounds and vibrations of communication within each cultural reality. For example, a major word of power in Greek is *Io Evoe*, which cannot be exactly translated, just like *amen* in a Christian prayer. *Io Evoe*, by itself, (roughly meaning "yea!") has special power and helps focus the energy of that spell.

There is also something to the power of what is called *twilight language*—language that affects the unconscious mind at a deeper spiritual level, though it may not be understandable to the conscious mind. Consider the power of the Latin Catholic Mass, remembering that most do not understand the Latin spoken during the ritual. Thus the twilight languages of Greek, Latin, and Egyptian used in these spells are to help move your focus and energies into the spiritual realm.

The best part of these spells is that they are practical and they have been used with success. So much that happens between you and your dog is subtle, unspoken, and, we think, psychic. Dogs *know* when you need them and when you are happy or scared. There is a deep and powerful unconscious magical link between humans and dogs. These spells just tap into this in a way that anyone can use to help their dog and themself. Do you need to open your life for a new dog or bond with your new dog or help heal, protect, or encourage your dog? There are spells in this book that do these things and much more.

We want to stress that anyone can do these spells! They use simple, easy-to-get materials and will benefit everyone who uses them in a positive manner when done with focus, belief, and sincerity. The key is, of course, your deep and evolving bond with your dog. These spells were written to add a deeper spiritual dimension to your relationship with your wonderful dog. How magical is that?

We know that you will infuse every bit of dog magic and each spell experience with a love for our canine companions without whom we would not be the humans we are. The heart of this book is that each dog is a hero, a friend, and a spiritual teacher and guide. Each dog embodies:

Beauty without Vanity
Strength without Insolence,
Courage without Ferocity,
and all the Virtues of Man without his Vices.
—Lord Byron (dedication to his dog, Boatswain)

Chapter Two

Your Spirit Dog

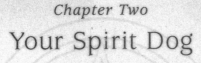

Invoking & Finding
Your Dog Familiar

In the beginning, there was *dog*.

At least this is what our dog thinks (just ask him). Is it a coincidence that *dog* is god spelled backward? Dog owners don't think so. Our dog is certainly divine in our home and just look at all those "Dog is My Copilot" bumper stickers out there. Some cultures in the world proclaim the "primal Dog Spirit" as their divine ancestor. In ancient Mongolia, for example, people venerate the "divine dog" as their original tribal ancestor. Friends who recently returned from Mongolia reported that dogs are treated like beloved family members there.

The Creator Dog

In Australia, the dingo is a sacred animal with its own "dreaming" or magical power as a sacred ancestor spirit. In the outback, we visited powerful and sacred dog dreaming sites. Even today dingoes are given skin names, which are human nicknames, demonstrating they are considered family members. The same applies in our home where our dog is given such sacred names as "bread stealer" and "stealth poodle" for his sneaky ways.

What dog doesn't like digging up old bones and gnawing endlessly on the stinky things? We would often find exotic items in the yard and wonder where the heck Thor had found them and how old they were. Dogs everywhere enjoy games like find the bone, chase the bone, and chew the bone. Maybe this explains Xolotl.

In Aztec mythology, the dog god Xolotl stole ancient bones from the underworld and brought them up to our world to help fashion a new race of man, thus aiding in the creation of our race. One wonders if he resisted chewing on them first.

Many cultures certainly viewed dogs as divine. I know our dog sees us as his responsibility and gets all barky if we don't stay together when hiking. In our home we often joke "how did we ever live without our dog?" and emotionally, we feel there is truth to this.

Apparently we are not alone in this feeling. There are many places where people *didn't* exist without dogs. In North America there is a Cherokee tribe that proclaims a dog is a founder of the tribe. According to myth, ancient Rome would have never existed without Lupa, the divine wolf mother of the twin founders, Romulus and Remus. An evil king forced the twins' abandonment, and they were suckled, saved, and protected by Lupa. These twins then went on to found the city of Rome and throw off the tyranny of the evil king. Since then, the wolf was a divine symbol of Rome. Romans always honored this divine "ancestor helper" as well as the "children of the wolf"—dogs.

Wolves seem to have a habit of raising, caring for, and protecting divine heroes, founders of civilizations, and so on. The ancient divine Germanic hero Siegfried was abandoned at birth and raised by a she-wolf. Tu Kueh, the mythic hero who prehistorically founded the Turkic peoples, was raised by a "blue" she-wolf. Clearly it was a popular thing for divine wolves to do in the ancient world. It makes you wonder why we don't treat wolves and other wild canines better today.

Our dog thinks himself the lord of his domain (our house) and some dog gods in myth felt the same way about all creation. The universe was their divinely created off-leash area. In ancient China, Taoists say the creator of the world is Pan Ku, a cosmic being formed of the cosmic Yin and Yang within a shining egg. A legend says Pan Ku, the ancestor of all mankind, was a dog. The myth, in brief, is that Pan Ku took on the form of the God of Heaven to avenge himself against an enemy god. Through cleverness, the dog Pan Ku vanquished this bad god and received his reward, the hand of the daughter of the King of Heaven. Pan Ku was then transformed into a mostly human-looking being. Pan Ku and his divine bride then descended to earth and had many children, the beginning of the human race. Thus we are all half divine and half dog. This might explain why our dog sees us as fellow dogs.

Dogs are not just our creators in these myths; they also gave us the key to civilization. We have to agree. Our dog makes us more civilized for sure.

The Lakota Sioux have a legend that shows the close relationship between tribal people and dogs. The First Dog Spirit came to the First Man and Woman giving them the divine gift of puppies to help them survive. In return, said the First Dog, mankind must provide food and shelter to their dog companions. This is called the pact of fire.

We love this story. It ends with a clear command to never mistreat such divine helpers. We think the Humane Society should spread this myth around.

In many forms, the Dog Spirit also helped humanity survive by stealing fire and giving it to human beings. Apache and other Native American myths claim that Coyote stole fire from the creator, gave it to the human tribes, and suffered as a result of this kindness. Maybe this is why all dogs love to sit around a fire with us. Possibly their fireside howling is their way of letting us know we are only borrowing *their* fire.

Across the globe, the dog is a symbol of creation, beginnings, and renewal for humanity. Every new puppy brought home represents this new creation and new world of love and bonding, protection and creation. As we strive to create a loving and safe world for our puppy, it is comforting to know that the ancient myths say the Dog Spirit did the same for us. This is, indeed, a sacred bone of creation and, of course, puppy play.

Spells, Meditations & Charms

Spell to Find the Perfect Breed

There is a lot to consider when you are looking for the right breed for yourself or your family. It is important that you first think about your environment, your family's needs, and what your interests and desires are when considering a dog. It may be wise to narrow down the breeds of dog that best suit your lifestyle and then choose several to do this divination with.

Dogs come in all sizes, so you can easily find the perfect height and weight you desire in a dog. If you want a mixed breed, this is fine too. Using this form of divination will work in both cases. Choosing the right breed can be very difficult, especially with so many to pick from. Divination using a pendulum as the way to help narrow down your search can help you find the dog breed that will be just the right fit for you.

You will need:
+ A pendulum (or you may use any small item on a string)
+ A picture of each breed you think you might want
+ The Moon card from a tarot deck
+ Sea salt
+ A silver candle
+ Matches

Place the pictures of the dogs facedown on the table and mix them up so you don't know which picture is what. Put the Moon card faceup above the dog pictures and sprinkle sea salt around all the pictures to make a circle. Concentrate on the cards and then say:

> *I want to know,*
> *I want to choose*
> *The best breed for me*
> *And my new dog, too.*
>
> *Be gone all confusion,*
> *Be gone all distractions,*
> *Like a moonbeam with focus*
> *And we take action.*

Now light the silver candle and say:

> *A special dog for me*
> *I feel you through the gate of the moon,*
> *Come now closer*
> *You will see soon.*

Pick up the pendulum, wave it through the candle three times, and say:

> *Oh Artemis, Diana, Hekate,*
> *My dog familiar be brought down to me*

Through the gate,
Let me see
As I will.
So mote it be.

Hold the pendulum in your right hand and rest your elbow on the table to keep the pendulum steady. Place it over each picture. If the pendulum goes in a circle over a picture, that is a yes to that dog breed. If the pendulum swings in a straight line that is a no. If the pendulum picks more than one dog, then you can repeat the divination with the pendulum to narrow down your choices. When the pendulum has narrowed the choices down to give a yes to only one picture, then turn it over to see what dog breed is right for you. Now say:

Dog of my dreams
Flew through the moon
Come now closer
You will soon do as I will.
So mote it be you will soon be part of me.

Blow out the candle and thank the moon goddess. Soon you will be united.

Inviting a Dog into Your Life Spell

Getting the right dog into your life takes a little bit of magic. It is important to get this right since both of you will be living together for many years to come. Sometimes a dog might just unexpectedly show up in your life—a stray, a gift, or just out of the blue a special dog shows up. These types of dogs are special soulmates. They picked you specifically.

However, sometimes you may have to call to a dog, invoke that special dog in your life, and go find it. Does this mean you can't have a soulmate dog? Of course not. If you pick your own dog you can get a soulmate, too. Inviting a dog takes a little bit of magic, but this spell could do the trick.

You will need:
+ Dog dishes
+ Dog food
+ A red dog toy
+ A dog whistle
+ A leash

Do this spell by your front door. Open the door a bit first, fill one dish with water, and say:

I invite you by the water of my love.

Fill the other dish with dog food and say:

I invite you by the earth of protection and caring.

Take the red toy and wave it over the bowls. Now say:

I invite you by fire of play and joy.

Blow the dog whistle or bark and then say:

I invite you by air of song and barks.

Now say:

We are twin stars, you and me.
I bless these gifts for you to receive.
You are for me, I am for you,
Come, O come by the name Pan Ku.

Pick up the leash, hold it in your hands, and say:

Bound together, never apart,
Bound to the end right from the start.
Commit to me, I commit to thee,
Our love is one,
So mote it be.

Soon the search for your special dog will end. You and your soulmate dog will be united. Make sure to give your new dog all these items.

Pick of the Litter Spell

Congratulations! You found the perfect litter of puppies, but now the hard part: Which puppy belongs to you? Once you make your choice, you can take home your little bundle of joy and then it will be all yours. But which one should it be? How are you going to make the final selection? Chanting these incantations to yourself while placing your hand on each of the puppies will help you let the right one in. You will know which puppy is meant to be yours while you chant this:

Inu-sama,*
Canine star,
I call your spirit
Near or far.
I am yours,
You are mine,
I call you by
The soul divine,
Inu-chan* kuru.*

Now place your hand on each puppy in turn and whisper:

Inu, inu,* which one is you?
Which one of you
Belongs to me?
Come, my love, help me see.

The warmest puppy is likely yours. But to make sure take the puppy in both of your hands and lift it up so your noses touch. Look into the puppy's eyes and say silently:

> *By my love*
> *You are mine.*
> *We are joined*
> *By power divine.*

Hold the puppy next to your heart, saying:

> *We are meant to be together.*
> *We are joined for all time.*
> *Let our love shine,*
> *Inu-chan dozo yoroshiku.**

Pet the puppy and feel if this is the best dog for you. Remember that this is a commitment for life and that you will need to take good care of your dog. It, in return, will take care of you. If the puppy licks you and snuggles into you this is a good sign. Sit the puppy in your lap and rock them until it falls asleep, if the puppy just closes its eyes this is okay too. Say to yourself:

> *As I rock you to sleep,*
> *Our dreams will be the same.*
> *We will belong together,*
> *Never to part.*

You are my puppy
Right from the start,
Inu-chan—yata!*

Now take your sweet little bundle home.

> ** Translation (Japanese): Inu-sama = Dog God; Inu-*
> *chan = beloved dog; Kuru = Come; Inu (pronounced*
> *ee-nu) = dog; Dozo yoroshiku = honored to know you;*
> *Yata = There it is!*

Magical Dog Name Meditation

Do you want to peer into the hidden world of your dog to find out the name you should bestow upon it? You can know what it knows and begin to think, sense, and feel who it is with one magical word of power, or so it is said. According to venerable magical books, all animals have "a secret name," especially animals that are magical companions. The secret and hidden name for dogs is MALOP.*

To use this "name of power" to discover what name your dog wants, simply whisper it to your dog three times and ask for dog wisdom. Then say:

Wyrd Sisters** three
Spin your web around me.
Through earth and sky

Open the eye.
I see the hidden
So it is written.

If your dog stares at you or lies at your feet, close your eyes and open your mind to receive the name you should give your loyal dog. If your dog walks away, it does not want to share now, try later.

> * From *The Crone's Book of Magical Words* by Valerie Worth
>
> ** Wyrd Sisters is one of the titles of the Three Fates

New Dog Love Visualization

You and your dog need to develop a special bond that is un-conditional love. A simple spell of intent will make your bond stronger. Loving and loyalty works both ways. Underlying this is trust, because without trust it is difficult to have a loving re-lationship. This simple spell can strengthen your new love for each other and that is a beautiful thing.

You will need:
+ A small bit of your dog's fur and your own hair
+ A red thread
+ Seeds from any flower
+ A white candle

+ Matches
+ A small flowerpot with dirt in it

Do this spell on a nice day when you and your dog are alone. Light the candle and say:

> *New love blossom,*
> *New love grow,*
> *New love is here*
> *This I know.*
> *Our bond is eternal*
> *Let love flow.*
> *Amo, amas, amamus.**

Take the thread and wrap it three times around both bits of hair and tie it with a knot. Hold this in your right hand, put your left arm around your dog, and visualize white light surrounding both of you in pure love.

Then, while looking at your dog, take the seeds in your right hand, and say:

> *You're bound to me*
> *And I to thee.*
> *We two seeds*
> *Are now one life,*
> *Full of love,*

Free of strife.
So may it be.

As the white light surrounds you, meditate on you and your dog's bond. Surround yourself in harmony. Now imagine both your hearts are molding into one. As you start to open up your eyes plant the tied hair deep in the pot and the seeds with it. Cover with earth and say:

I am bound to thee
And you to me.
Together in power,
Love's divine flower.
Now and forever,
So may it be.

Blow out the candle, water the flower seeds, and go out for a walk with your loving dog. Keep watering the flower seeds until they grow and bloom. Now you are truly bound with love forever.

* Translation (Latin): Amo, amas, amamus = I love, you love, we (together) love.

Always Come Back to Me Spell

Some dogs like to wander off to someplace new, but what if your dog gets lost when it goes on a stroll and can't find its way back home? Whatever the reason for your dog getting lost, it could be a potential nightmare for you. Helping your dog to never leave home sweet home without you may need a little magical help. This charm will help keep your dog from getting lost so it can always safely find its way home to you.

You will need:

+ Any "good luck charm" that is metal and small enough to put on a collar with the rest of your dog's tags, maybe a star or a small sun or a clover symbol
+ You will be drawing the rune for the Norse god Tyr on the charm. It looks like this: ↑
+ A green pen
+ A green candle
+ Matches

Take the charm and place it next to the candle. Now light the candle and put a simple arrow symbol on the charm with the green pen. Light the candle and say, while looking into your dog's eyes:

Tyr, hear, always stay.
You will never run away.
Always be by my side,
Never vanish, never hide.
If you do someday run free,
Always return to me.

Put the charm on your dog's collar, put it on your dog, and say:

On the earth
He does roam.
Bring me to him,
Bring him home.
It is meant to be,
He will come to me.
Make him see
That near me
Is where he ought to be.
By Thor's hammer
Protected be.

Blow out the candle and go out for a walk.

Chapter Three

Dog Love

Bonding With
& Loving Your Dog

Some might disagree, but we believe that no one loves us more than our dog. From the first day we brought him home, he has leaped in delight when he sees us, no matter what. That is pure devotion. They say a dog's heart is as big as the world, and you dog lovers out there know what we mean.

We also know that our dog is, well, a "dog." He has, shall we say, several girlfriends and a couple of boyfriends. When he is "in the mood" we just shove them outside and ignore the ruckus.

This is clearly why historically dogs are symbols of both devotional love as well as sexual love. It is also why we neutered and spayed our dogs, though it never seems to stop the shenanigans.

In myth and folklore, dogs are symbols of sexual power and symbols of that deep transcendent love found in committed relationships, friendships, and spiritual sharing across cultures.

Dog Love

No dog was more loving than Hachiko, the famous dog of Tokyo, and now he exists as an honored spirit. Hachiko was utterly devoted to his owner and walked him to his commuter train every day and met him every night. His owner died at work and never came home. For the rest of his life, Hachiko came to the station every morning and every evening and was increasingly loved by all until he passed away.

In Shinto, the Animist religion of Japan, such a transcendent love and spirit is honored. Many consider Hachiko a powerful spirit to this day. They even created a statue in his honor. Hachiko's statue is a famous shrine and a popular place for friends and lovers to meet.

Our personal bond with our dog is so deep it sometimes amazes us. He knows when we are sad and comforts us; he knows when we are joyful and plays with us. It is a selfless love indeed, and it began from the first moment we got our new puppy and bonded with it, cuddling the small black ball of fur for hours. We believe that kind of love is spiritual.

One example of this powerful, bonding love magic is found in Mongolia. When taking a puppy from a mother dog, the mother dog is honored and fed by those adopting the puppy. A light blue ceremonial scarf covered with auspicious symbols is given to the family. Forever after, that dog is considered a true family member, like a new child.

This loving embrace of a dog as family member carries over into the afterlife in many cultures. In ancient Egypt, dogs were shown doing everything with their humans and, like humans, were buried with food and other comforts as one would a family member.

We believe the same way. We bought a cement dog statue resembling our dog. Now he is very old, so we know that when he passes we too will bury him with his toys, his collar, and some treats under this statue. We know that the love we feel for him and he for us will continue. Some kinds of dog magic never change.

What of romantic love? Dogs always love us, and that means they want to make sure that we make good romantic choices. Recently a friend dating a nice guy broke up with him because, as she told us, "My dog hated him, what could I do?" Even dog spirits need to give their approval, it would appear.

Most know of the tradition of a newlywed groom carrying the bride over the threshold, but did you know that there is a dog magic element involved? In ancient times, people would have a magical spirit dog guarding the entryway of a home. The groom would carry the bride over to alert the Dog Spirit guardian that this was the new mistress of the home.

Many cultures used domestic dog charms or small dog guardian images in the home to protect the family and the marriage. Even today we can see this in the old Hebrew tradition of keeping a small dog image with your marriage certificate!

Dogs (and other canines) have been associated with sex forever. Even today we call sexually adventurous men and women "foxes," "wolves," and "dogs" and being a "hound dog" or "sniffing around" are actually very old idioms of sexual interest along with "wolf whistles," "dogging" someone, and "woof."

There are a number of dog gods and divine dog heroes embodying the sexual urge, and none is as popular as Old Man Coyote, the ubiquitous Native American trickster spirit that used his wiles and silver tongue to mate with many women. In some instances, he is the genetic founder of a tribe. In many Native American myths, the people were so convinced of the coyote's unbridled libido they depicted him with a huge penis swung over his shoulder or so big that he had to carry it in a pack! There are many racy stories about Coyote and his exploits.

Sometimes sexually aggressive people really *were* dogs. The Greeks called were-dogs *Cynanthropes* ("dog people") or *Cynocephali* ("dog headed"), and the existence of "dog people" is a common idea in many cultures. *Cyn* means "dog" in Greek, by the way. Such dog men (or women) were universally viewed as lustier than normal people. The same applies to werewolves and were-foxes, and is in the description of most forms of shape-shifters. In Japan and Korea, fox spirits and wolf people have a history of seducing and even marrying humans.

We know how lusty dogs can get, but did you know during the dark ages, the devil was said to visit witches in the form of a black dog and have sexual congress with them? This might be traced to the goddess Hecate's black dog, also associated with wild sexuality. Our dog is a black dog and while we are pretty sure he is not the devil (usually), he certainly is romantically wild sometimes.

Dogs are associated with many erotically inclined gods. This includes the lusty gods Pan, Silvanus, and Faunus (the Roman Pan). Faunus was famous for the wild ritual of fertility called Lupercalia or "wolf festival." In this celebration, satyr-like men wearing strips of wolf fur chased and lightly whipped naked women hoping to conceive. This was considered a Roman highlight of the year and at the beginning of the festival priests sacrificed a dog to help unleash fertility and wild sexuality.

Love and sex are topics that preoccupy much of our lives. Of course, as usual, dogs sit right there in the middle of things. These themes of love and lust remind us that we are still animals, and our loving dogs are there to remind us every day that this can be a good thing.

Spells, Meditations & Charms

Imprinting with a New Puppy Spell

When a new puppy enters your life, it is a bit traumatized. Where did Mommy go? What is this new bright world? What are all these new scents? *Waaaaa!* It is just a baby after all, and you just adopted it. Make the adoption official with this magical exercise. This first imprinting with your new partner is the most crucial.

You will need:

+ A small, deep blue soft cloth or blanket made of natural fabric, soft cotton, or wool (a baby blanket is perfect)
+ Some rose water

Important: Sleep with this cloth or blanket close to your skin at least one night before you get the puppy. Before you go to sleep, hold the blanket close and burn calming incense (jasmine is perfect) while thinking happy puppy thoughts.

At twilight or early evening, go outside with the blanket and stand quietly, thinking peaceful thoughts. Breathe deeply. Completely relax. Place the blanket about you. Feel your joy at getting a new puppy. Surround yourself with calming blue light. Say:

> *The lair is safe,*
> *The night brings peace.*
> *All stress and sorrow*
> *Now release.*
> *Om.*

Sprinkle a little rose water over the blanket and the area. Chant *om* softly as you do so. See the light of calm spirit cover all.

Later, after the puppy feeds from your hands and is sleepy, sit in a dimly lit place. Face north. Put the blanket on your lap and place the new puppy on it.

Stroke the puppy slowly, softly, from nose to tail, and say:

From sorrow be clear.
Know I am here
To love and protect you
And banish all fear,
(Whisper the dog's new name).

Repeat this as many times as you like. See loving, calming blue energy enter and calm your puppy. As you hold your new puppy hum softly these words:

You are mine now,
You are mine now,
You are mine now.
Here is peace.
Om.

Hold and love the little baby as long as you like. When it is put in its puppy bed, repeat the last chant while your puppy sleeps on this blanket. This will be its special calming blanket for life.

Spell to Deepen the Bond with Your Dog

A dog is a friend for life, one of the few stable things in an otherwise often shaky and confusing world. The bond between a dog and owner (and vice versa) is a sacred one and has been ever since the first wolf pups choose to hang out with humans. This is a very old and powerful spell used to cement the bonds of loyalty and love between a human and a dog. This spell will work for an adopted puppy or for a dog that already reached maturity. Here is a relationship you can count on, even when life gets "ruff."

You will need:
* A nice piece of meat or a special treat
* A copper plate or bowl
* A pinch of dirt

On a full moon, gather your loving dog to you. Place the meat on the copper plate and set it on a table. Closely breathe three times on the meat, seeing your spirit light entering the meat. Then say:

> *By bond and breath,*
> *By love;*
> *By bond and breath,*
> *By joy;*
> *By bond and breath,*
> *By loyalty;*
> *Canum et ludens.**
> *So mote it be.*

Take the dirt and sprinkle it around the dog's bowl. As you do so, say:

Here he's rooted, here he'll stay,
Abiding with me, never going away.
Green magic, (your dog's name).

Let your dog lick the hand that the dirt was in. While your dog licks your hand, say:

Here I am rooted, here I will stay,
Together with him forever I say,
Green magic, (your name).

Your dog is probably very interested in the food by now. Feed your dog with love and an open heart. You are now spirit bound and will stick together through all. You are partners. Have fun.

* Translation (Latin): Canum et ludens = Dog Joy.

Loyalty & Love Visualization

You and your dog have a special bond of undying loyalty and unconditional love. Pure loyalty will only make your bond become stronger. Loving and loyalty work each way for both of you. Underlying this is trust, because without trust it is almost impossible to have a loyal and loving relationship. A meditation for the both of you can strengthen this loyalty and love for each other, and that is a beautiful thing.

You will need:
+ Your dog
+ A staff or wand, something previously charged magically is best
+ Cinnamon
+ A park or wooded place where you can mark the earth

With a deep breath, chant *om*. Draw a large pentagram in the earth, large enough for you and your dog. As you do so, chant *ah*.

Bring your dog with you into the pentagram and seal it by sprinkling cinnamon clockwise about you both, chanting *hum*.

Sit within this magical circle. Hold your dog in your lap or as much as you can if you own a big dog. Sit calmly. Put a pinch of cinnamon on your crown and on your dog's crown and chant:

*Om ah hum**

Pet your dog with your right hand and put your left around it. When your dog is calm, close your eyes and visualize white light surrounding both of you, bathing you in pure love. As the white light surrounds you meditate on you and your dog's favorite place. Visualize both your dog and yourself as beings of pure interlocking energy. Now mediate on the fact that you are both one in the white light. Surround yourself in harmony. Listen to both of your hearts by placing one hand on your dog's heart and one on yours. Now see a silver cord connect and tie your hearts to one another. Keep doing this until you feel the cord tightening and your hearts molding into one.

Visualize this glowing heart within the pentagram you have cast. Inhale and feel this pentagram become absorbed within you both. Open your eyes anytime and hug your dog in your arms. Chant:

Om ah hum

Erase the pentagram and leave a pinch of cinnamon as an offering for the spirits of this place. Go about your day.

* Translation (Sanskrit): Hum = Buddhist mantra or vibration of heavy protection and purification; Om ah hum = Mind, voice, heart.

Getting Along with Other Pets & People in a New Home Chant

Everyone living in your home already knows each other's strengths and weaknesses. There are well-established relationships among all of the family members. So, it is hard for a new dog to know how it will be part of the family. Being introduced into a new home is difficult for even the friendliest dog, as family members already have their territories mapped out in the home. Intruding into the territory of another makes it even more difficult for the newest member of the family to feel at home. A new dog will need care and love to learn how to be part of the family.

Helping the newest family member to feel at home may need a little boost and this meditation can help with that.

You will need:
+ The dog's bed
+ All the new dog's belongings
+ Pictures of all the family members in your home
+ A meal for all the members of the family, any kind of food everyone likes is fine

Have your new dog lie in its bed and everyone in the family sit around taking turns petting the new family member. Everyone closes their eyes and meditates on the new dog getting along with everyone and everyone getting along with it. Have the other animals in the home join you too, and chant over and over again:

*A home in harmony is bliss—hau.**

Now each of you pass around the dog's belongings and chant:

With each of these belongings
We welcome you.
This our potlatch
From us to you.
Hau, hau, hau.

Gather around the dinner table to have your first meal together, and before you put the new puppy's food down, say:

Bless this food.
Bless our newest member.
We now have one heart home
Now and forever.

Take a photo of all of you together and this is your new family picture. When it is developed, hang the picture near where the dog will sleep. Now everyone should enjoy the family's first meal together.

* Translation (Lakota Sioux): Hau = Greetings.

Dog Romance Success in Breeding Spell

Finding a suitable mate for your dog is very important. Some matches aren't made in heaven. Most purebreds have some sort of genetic problem due to lines of inbreeding. Sometimes it is really the luck of the draw, but you need to narrow down which dog you choose to breed your dog with to result in the healthiest puppies and not pass down genetic problems.

Finding your dog the perfect mate for breeding may take help using divination. To do this type of divination, you will need to select a few dogs that you want to breed your dog with. Will your dog like what dog you pick as the future mother or father of the puppies to be? This is where divination comes in and puppy love blooms.

You will need:
+ A die (one of a pair of dice)
+ Colored paper: pink if your dog is female, and blue if your dog is male
+ A red rose
+ A red pen
+ A red candle
+ Matches

Choose the correct color paper and write on it the names of dogs you picked for possible breeding. Put by each name any number from one to six. Now draw the astrological symbol of Venus ♀ over the names.

Light the candle and say:

Venus bonum fortuna.*
Fill with zest,
Spice it up,
Amore est.*

Then place the die on top of the paper. With your dog on your lap, wave the red rose over your dog and say:

Goddess of love, goddess of passion,
Find us a dog that will breed with compassion.

Successful breeding come to me
By Venus and Adonis may it be.
Omnia amore est.*

Now roll the die on the paper and the number that comes up is the right dog for the job.

Look deeply into your dog's eyes and tell him or her you found it a special friend. Offer the rose to the goddess Venus and then place it out of your dog's reach but near where it sleeps.

* Translation (Latin): Venus bonum fortuna = Great fortune through Venus; Amore est = Love is!; Omnia amore est = All this is love.

Making Your Dog Your Familiar

Shamans, sorcerers, witches, and other magic makers often have familiars, or pet friends, as part of their magical reality. Such power pets can help in countless ways of spirit, but forming an initial bond is important and, according to ancient lore, traditional. Here is a spell for making your dog into your familiar.

You will need:
+ A sharp pin cleaned with some rubbing alcohol
+ Your dog's favorite dinner food
+ A clear crystal
+ Rosemary

+ A white candle
+ Matches

Do this on a full moon. The moon should be in view through a window or you can do this outside.

Walk around your area with your clear crystal. As you circle about sprinkle rosemary and say three times:

*Apos pantos kakodaimonos.**

Be gone all negative spirits, powers, and feelings.
By the mother of the mountain
And mother of the sea,
Mother of animals,
So mote it be.

Now sit face-to-face with your dog and be silent. Lean your forehead against your dog's forehead and open your mind and heart with love and caring. Silently ask your dog if it wants to enter into the sacred pact of the familiar. Commune.

If all seems well, take the pin and prick your left thumb. Use the pin to write your dog's name on the candle. Drip three drops of blood into the dog food, saying:

By Crone and Mother and Maid,
By star wolf, moon wolf, sun wolf red,
The pact is given and laid.

By the heart and the head.
*Kyon, Kyon, Kyon.**

Take up the rosemary and burn it, waving smoke over you and your dog as you now chant:

> (Your dog's name) *and I are one.*
> *Our minds, our hearts are one.*
> *Our bodies are one.*

Give your dog its food, if it readily eats, your pet is now your familiar. If not, it is not yet time. When finished, repeat the communing and then end as you will… Maybe with a howl?

* *Translation (Greek): Apos pantos kakodaimonos = Be*
gone all demons; (Old Greek) Kyon = Dog.

Chapter Four

Dog Healing

Healing & Being Healed
Through Your Dog

We will never forget the winter everyone in our home got the flu. One after another, we got sick. Often all we could do was lay on the couch and moan. Our dog lay right on top of us the whole time, passing from one person to the other. He got up when we did (seldom), and he ate, drank water, and stayed with us. We agreed he was literally healing us. We joked about "laying on of paws" healing. The truth is, we believe he did help heal us. Nothing has felt quite as healing as the love and energy that dog poured into us. I know every dog owner has a similar story.

Healing Dog

Most people recognize the healing power of companion or "service" dogs in today's world. This power to heal, comfort, and guide people with mental or physical issues was even more recognized in the ancient world. The Greeks, Egyptians, Chinese, and Hittites thought that the dog spirit protected not only from terrestrial enemies, but also from evil spirits that were seen as the cause of all disease. If a person felt the onset of these spirits, they often had a magical dog or a dog charm nearby.

Have you ever had a dog lick your cut? I remember once gardening and slicing my palm on a thorn. My dog was nearby and licked it. I figured I'd wash it later, but I forgot. The next day I was amazed to find it basically healed and free of infection.

Since ancient Egypt a dog lick has been considered by some to be the equivalent of antibiotic cream. This likely adds to the mythic connection between dogs and healing in many cultures. There is actually some proof to this belief. Dog saliva contains lysozyme, an enzyme that kills some bacteria, histidines that ward off infections, and other chemicals that promote healing. Historical accounts from ancient Greece and Rome tell about dogs accompanying soldiers into battle and being used to clean wounds by healers. Considering that none of these people possessed antibiotics, likely they were on to something.

The greatest healer of the ancient world was supposedly Aesculapius, a Greek demigod, often depicted accompanied by a dog, his divine helper and protector. At Epidaurus, his sanctuary and place of origin, and at every *asklepieion* ("healing shrine") we visited in Greece, statues of his magical dog helper are still found along with the divine serpent crawling up his staff, a symbol of medicine. Sacred dogs were always present at these shrines, and are considered part of the healing process. Maybe, we can surmise, from their healing licks, but also because of the psychological and spiritual assistance they provide.

The Celtic god of healing was Nodens. His symbol was also a dog. In England, images of Nodens and his dog have been found on offering plaques left by grateful pilgrims healed from a variety of afflictions. These temples of Nodens were healing centers much like the *asklepieion* in Greece.

The dog, a healing power in ancient Celtic society, is often depicted in images and on offerings found at healing springs all over the United Kingdom and Europe. The goddess Epona, best known as a Celtic horse goddess, is often depicted holding her sacred dog in her lap. The Celts invoked Epona for fertility and healing for animals and humans. Many healing female deities are shown with sacred dogs.

The god Cunomaglus (Great Hound Lord) is known from an inscription at his temple in the United Kingdom. Truly dog healing magic was a huge theme in the ancient Celtic world where, even today, if you visit, you will see a truly dog-crazy nation. Look at the amazing Westminster dog show.

Divine dog healing was also all the rage in the ancient Near East. There the dog was associated with many healing goddesses such as Ninisinna, Bau (or Baba), Gula, and Nin-karak. From prehistoric Sumerian culture through Akkadian, Babylonian, and Chaldean times, healing goddesses were commonly depicted with divine healing dogs.

Often a dog image was venerated as the actual embodiment of the healing goddess. For example, during excavations at Isin, the ancient city sacred to the healing goddess Ninisinna, archaeologists discovered plaques with images of dogs, a statue of a kneeling figure hugging a dog, and small clay dog amulets inscribed with prayers to the goddess for healing.

We were lucky enough to see some of these items at the Museum of Anatolian Civilizations (*Anadolu Medeniyetleri Muzesi*) in Turkey. We thought that the people hugging the healing dog goddess looked a lot like family pictures of us hugging our dog. It is nice to know people have been hugging dogs for health for ages. We know that dog hugs make us feel better.

Of course we can continue going on and on about healing dogs. Let's face it, dogs are loving and trustworthy, and you'd trust a doctor who had a friendly dog, right?

In Catholic churches, even today healing dogs abound. Mother Mary is often shown with a dog, representing love and compassion. Saint Domino, the saint who heals diseases (especially rabies), has a dog as his symbol. Shrines of many saints who have a dog as a symbol, such as Saint Guinefort, are famous for healing as well.

Who does not immediately love babies and puppies? Having a baby is never painless for people, we know from experience. Yet when our friend's poodle had pups, it was fast and seemed almost painless, even having a litter of ten puppies. That easy birthing is a powerful magic that mankind has noticed throughout history. This explains why divine dogs are often invoked to ease and protect women and babies during childbirth.

The fearsome Hekate is a goddess who helps with childbirth, and as such, her dogs became a symbol of easy and safe birth. In Japan, worshipers pray for an easy and safe childbirth at shrines to the watery kami or child-god Suijin (also called Suitengu), whose symbol is a dog.

We visited such a Suitengu shrine before the birth of our son. We rubbed the large metal magical dog's nose and received an amulet to bring to the hospital. Who really knows if it helped, but nurses at our son's birth in Tokyo were all very impressed we went there. Many temples and shrines in the ancient world that were connected with dogs served as spiritual (and at times, actual, as in Greek *asklepieion*) hospitals. In this way, the loving and patient dog spirit was and is helper and guardian of healing and helping adults and new human pups.

Spells, Meditations & Charms

Receiving Dog Healing Meditation

Are you sick? Down in the dumps? Whatever it is that is making you unwell, your dog can help comfort and heal you. Dogs for thousands of years worldwide have been present to heal and comfort the sick. Dogs will naturally lie by you when you need care, and they won't leave your side until you get up and are feeling better. Giving healing energy comes naturally to dogs, and receiving healing through meditation with your dog is extremely comforting.

You will need:
+ Salt
+ Pine or cedar branch or pine or cedar incense
+ A dog brush

Sprinkle salt around where you are going to perform your healing and then say:

> *I start the healing*
> *To connect with the chakras as one,*
> *And now I will receive your*
> *Divine energy to get*
> *Better and once again*
> *We will run in the sun.*

Now burn the incense or wave the branch and say:

> *By the healing sound of Aum**
> *And the healing sound of Ha,**
> *Aum-Ha.*

Brush the dog three times and say three times:

> *Sickness out*
> *Night and day,*

Sickness away
Aum-Ha.

Invite your dog to lie next to you as closely as you can until both of you are comfortable. Keep your heads near each other. Put one hand on your dog and the other where you feel the most discomfort. You will be tapping into your chakras with this meditation.

Close your eyes and breathe in and out rhythmically until you feel relaxed. Then you are going to vibrate the sound of the chakra associated with the part of your body that needs healing. If you are sick all over, maybe with the flu, vibrate the sounds of all the chakras, from the base to the top. As you do this, feel and see the loving green healing energy of your dog filling you.

The root chakra starts at the anus and the chant is *Lam*.

The second chakra starts at the lower back and the chant is *Vam*.

The third chakra starts at the stomach and the chant is *Ram*.

The fourth chakra starts at the heart and the chant is *Yam*.

The fifth chakra starts at the throat and the chant is *Ham*.

The sixth chakra starts at the "third eye" of your head and the chant is *Om*.

The seventh chakra starts at the top of your head and there is no sound but the "silent sound" of all.

Chant the chakra sounds until you start feeling better. Thank your dog with a hug and give it back some energy and maybe take a nap together. Make sure you both eat well when you can.

> * Translation (Sanskrit): Aum = Om, the force of Creation.
> Ha is the seed-mantra for the Endless Manifestation, the
> other seed-mantra sounds activate the chakras indicated.
> All chakra mantras are pronounced with long A: Example:
> YAM = Yi-AY-MM; HAM = H-AY-MM.

Restful Night Sleep for You & Your Dog Spell

Sometimes with a new puppy, an older dog, or simply for a restless dog, sleep is a problem. We all know what it's like when you have to go to work and your dog wakes you up several times at night. Calming this energy can help both you and your dog sleep well and will be good for both of you. While the goddess Hecate may seem forbidding, she is the protector of dogs, guide of the pathways of waking and sleeping, and lady of night and rest. Call upon her for restful sleep.

You will need:
+ Chamomile tea
+ A small ceramic bowl of salt water

+ Lavender incense
+ A purple candle
+ Matches

Make the chamomile tea and set it on your night table along with the salt water. Light the incense and candle and say:

Io Evoe*
Come, O gentle Hekate,
Protector of dogs,
People too,
Bring restful sleep,
We petition you.
Praise Nyx.*

Before your dog goes to sleep, think of a calm, quiet night and letting go of stress. Drink the tea, giving a little to your dog as well. Cuddle with your dog and as you do dip your ring finger in the salt water, touch your dog's head, and hum a sleepy time tune to this invocation:

You are that, you are all.
With all you rise,
With all you fall.
Life and death,
Night and day,
Pain and pleasure,

Ever-changing play.
In the center of all
Is great release.
You are the center of all,
Now go to sleep.

When the tea is gone and the incense is done, wish your dog a good night and blow out the candle. Have a restful sleep.

  * *Translation (Greek): Io Evoe = (no direct translation, but this is closest) Yea. Hail. Holy; Nyx = Night.*

Spell for Successful Dog Travel

Time for the family vacation, which of course includes the most important member—the dog. What would a vacation be without including the whole pack? Not going on vacation? Maybe the family dog or a new dog will be traveling alone or delivered by plane or some other means of transportation. No matter if your dog is traveling with you or not, having your dog travel is hard for everyone. Hermes watches out over dogs, so maybe his help is just what you both need. To ask for his help use this spell.

You will need:
+ Crumbled dog biscuits
+ A luggage tag
+ A pen

+ An orange candle
+ Matches or a lighter

Take the crumbled dog biscuits and hold them in your hand. Stand in the middle of the place where your dog will be sleeping and put the luggage tag, pen, candle, and matches at your feet. You will be sprinkling a little of the dog biscuit crumbs in each direction, and as you go around, say:

In the east:

> *By the winds about the world*
> *Ever whirling in their course*
> *Shared as the breath of every life,*
> *Which speaks all words of power.*

In the south:

> *By the fires of transformation*
> *That blazes and burns,*
> *That spirals and turns,*
> *That fills the darkness with shadow.*

In the west:

> *By the waters of wine-dark sea,*
> *Waves that shake the solid land,*
> *Ocean womb that brings forth life*
> *To rise and grow and change.*

In the west:

> *By the stones beneath our feet,*
> *By the wilderness of time,*
> *By the ancient name we invoke thee:*
> *Hermes, Hermes, Hermes.*

Write on the luggage tag the addresses where your dog will be coming from and then arriving to. Place it near the candle and say:

> *Hermes/Mercury, the god of traveling,*
> *Watch over my dog as he travels far*
> *Swiftly and painlessly, to you we sing*
> *Whether by air or train or car.*
> *Hermes of the crossroads—so may it be.*

Now blow out the candle and carry the tag with your dog or have the luggage tag attached to its bag or crate.

Keep Your Dog Healthy Meditation

A note of caution, if your dog seems really ill, take him or her to the veterinarian and get it checked out immediately. This mediation is to give your dog healing energy if it is a bit unwell. Having a sick dog is very sad, especially since dogs don't complain, and it is difficult to know how it is really feeling. Keeping it healthy is always of utmost importance and giving it healing love if it is ill, injured, or just under the weather will give you both a feeling of well-being.

You will need:
+ Some fresh grass
+ A small amethyst stone
+ A small onyx stone
+ Bowl of salt water

Start by sprinkling grass around your sick dog, saying:

> *Gaia, mother of animals,*
> *Lady of beasts,*
> *Protector of the wild ones,*
> *Mother of healing and love,*
> *Banish all illness*
> *From this your child.*

Place the amethyst in your right hand and the onyx in your left. Hold the stones above the places your dog is hurting or at the weakest part of its body. If it is a general problem, pet your dog from head to tail with the stones over and over. Try to breathe in and out with the same rhythm as your dog. As you breathe, visualize your dog's pain absorbed into the onyx and allowing the stone to hold all the negative energy of its disease or injury. When you no longer see the dark energy of your dog's hurt drawn into the onyx, put the onyx into the salt water. Using the healing power of the amethyst, still breathing as closely as you can to match your dog's breathing, visualize the amethyst's powerful energy transforming into a great beam of light to heal your dog. Place the amethyst into the salt water, take out both stones and go outside to pour the water into the earth.

Place both hands on the ground and say:

> *I am,*
> *You are,*
> *We are*
> *Gaia healing.*

Kiss your dog and visualize him or her feeling better soon.

Spells to Heal Dogs Who Have Suffered

Nothing is sadder than to see in the news or on television, or to hear a witness describing, a dog or dogs suffering. Maybe it is just seeing the horrible aftermath of a mistreated dog. Maybe you adopted a traumatized dog that needs help. Although the damage is done, you can start helping the healing process magically. Spells can be used directly with the dog next to you, or you can use a spell to heal a dog (or dogs) that you won't ever have in your arms. Either way, magic is powerful and can soothe not only the dog, but yourself as well. You may feel helpless, but in reality you are giving a wonderful gift, the gift of hope and healing.

You will need:

+ A green candle
+ A white candle
+ Matches
+ The abused or injured dog or a picture of the dog or dogs you want to heal
+ Some horsehair and/or a picture of your favorite horse

Light the candles and stare into the flame with the hurt dog or the photo of the dogs you want to heal lying next to you. Now place the horsehair and/or a horse picture next to the hurt dog or the photo. Place your palms open and toward the dog you want to heal (or the photo) and say:

> Epona, great Celtic goddess of healing,
> Protect and heal this dog's body and feeling.
> May you hold them in your arm
> To keep them from further harm.
> Curatio Sanat. *

Now touch the abused dog to be healed or the picture of the dog(s) that you want to ease the suffering of. Place both of your palms on the picture of the horse or hold the horsehair in your hand. Visualize that you are the goddess Epona riding her horse with the dog sitting on your lap and say:

Great Goddess Epona,
Riding a horse,
Ease the suffering
Of the dog in my lap.
Curatio sanat.

Have this supercharged healing energy run through you to your hands and into the dog. If working with a dog directly, stroke the dog gently with the horsehair.

Then burn the photo and/or the horsehair and eventually toss the ashes into running water. Blow out the candles

* Translation (Latin): Curatio Sanat = Heal and Cure.

Charm for Dog Healing: Issues of Appetite, Weight, Energy & So On

Sometimes all you need is a charm to help boost your dog's appetite, balance its weight, and/or moderate its energy. It can be frustrating, as well as confusing, not knowing what one should do when things are out of balance with your dog. If it is affecting your dog's health and you need to get your dog to eat, or it has a low (or too high) energy level or is losing weight, try this charm. Be sure that you take your dog to the vet in case it has an underlining health problem and may need medical care. However, a charm may help get your dog balanced again.

You will need:

+ A pin or a small knife
+ A tiny piece of your dog's favorite food or a treat
+ A yellow candle
+ Matches

At midday, have your dog close to you. Take the pin or a small knife and draw an infinity symbol ∞ on the treat.

Light the yellow candle, which is the chakra color for the stomach area and controls metabolism and energy. Have your dog lie on its back and rub its belly, tracing the infinity symbol over and over again gently with your fingers, saying:

> Balance, balance,
> Calm and peace.
> Balance, balance,
> Stress release.
> Balance, balance,
> Eating and energy.
> Balance, balance
> IAO*—so may it be.

Wave your dog's food or a treat over the flame eight times and feel it full of balancing yellow energy. Say:

> Strength and strong,
> Balance, balance.

Happy and glad,
Balance, balance.
IAO—so may it be.

Take the tiny piece of your dog's food and as you feed it, say:

Feel better,
Balance, balance.
Get well soon,
Balance, balance.
Healthy you will be,
Balance, balance.
IAO—so may it be.

Your dog should feel better in no time.

* Translation (Greek/Gnostic): IAO (pronounced EEEE
AHHHH OHHH) = HEAL—also can mean LIGHT.

Chapter Five

Dog Protection

Protecting & Being
Protected by Your Dog

When our dog was still a small, furry critter, we had a problem with wild animals coming from the woods behind our house and invading our yard. Raccoons, possums, wood rats, and crows would poop all over, tear up our son's toys, and just cause mayhem. Within a few days, our puppy had chased them all out and from then on did morning and nightly rounds of our property line, keeping every unwanted creature away by the force of his personality. Now that is dog magic. All dogs do this, it is in their blood, and this deep doggy-mission to protect extends into the spirit realm.

Dog Protection

The mandrake, a real and magically powerful root, was useful for sorcerers but was also capable of killing with a shriek when pulled from the ground. The old tomes had a solution; have a dog pull it out. Of course, the dog familiar is happy to do this because, as dog owners know, our dogs will do anything to protect us, even pull out dangerous roots. Dogs were (and are) common magical familiars for wizards, witches, and sorcerers. These dogs protected their magic workers from evil spirits, aided them in their spells, and helped them to see spirits. These companions help with divination and drive off all sorts of evil creatures, including unwelcome solicitors.

Dog magic was used in protecting places and people since Paleolithic times. Sad to say, dogs were sacrificed and buried under the entryways of temples, palaces, and homes for thousands of years, including church grims (guard dogs buried in the foundations of gothic churches). While this does indeed seem grim, it should be noted that this practice was replaced by either burying small spirit guard dog images with spells under the entryway of homes and temples or erecting dog guardian statues. This is why, even today, mansions often have dog statues protecting the entryway, though now they are just decoration. Once, however, these guardian dogs were serious business and even today stone or metal temple dogs, are very common sights in many countries.

Why dogs? The answer is: because dogs have always protected humanity. Wolves cohabitated with prehistoric tribes. They benefited by being fed and in return they protected humans from predators, thus our two species are bound symbiotically. This bond of loyalty, devotion, and protection is a sacred pact that exists today, extending into the spiritual realm. We certainly feel safer with our dog and often note that we see few ghosts, so it must be working.

All across Asia, "Lion Dogs" (*Shi* in Chinese and in Japanese,) guard temples, shrines, and holy spots in addition to palaces and important buildings. Something of a mythological blend of the lion and the massive guard dog, they are often called "Foo Dogs," meaning magic or power. The famous "snow lion" protector of Buddha and the symbol for Tibetan Buddhism is one such guardian spirit. Today we know them by their smaller version, the shih tzu.

Such sacred dog guards are often in pairs representing Yin and Yang. In myths, they protect people, gods, and towns from demonic or negative powers. Many Japanese festival *Kagura* (or sacred plays) depict the fight between an invading evil spirit or demon and the repelling of that evil by the loyal, tenacious Lion Dog guardians. In Bali, this lion dog is called Barong and fights off the evil witch-goddess Rangda in many plays, songs, and sculptures.

In our travels we notice such guard dogs in front of many temples and palaces. When we asked why their noses were worn down, we were told that everyone who enters must pet them for luck. *Of course,* we thought, *why wouldn't you pet such friendly dogs, especially if they were protecting you?*

Sometimes other magic canines protect people and temples, such as in Japan where special fox images protect shrines sacred to the mother goddess Inari and traditionally guarded the huge rice storehouses located at such shrines. Kitsune spirit statues are kept at homes and shrines to protect people, and the spirits are often depicted on amulets. When we visited a big Inari shrine with our infant son, an elderly woman ran out and gave us two small fox statues to protect our house and child. We still have those small images, and even now they smile at us.

Of course what we want protection from more than anything is death. There was a dog god long ago who did this and, when you finally did die, he protected you into the afterlife. Now *that* is a loyal dog spirit. We speak, of course, of Anubis (Anpu in Egyptian) the famous jackal or dog-headed god.

Oddly enough, dog spirits also guard the gate of death in Celtic mythology. Called "Dormarth" or "death's door" we still see these guardian dogs (or wolf dogs) on the Moon tarot card, still guarding that gate to the other side. (Why are they and other Celtic dog spirits guarding this moon gate? Because it is the gate of death, rebirth, and of the astral realm, the spirit-world.)

It is always good to have a dog guarding the gate "between the worlds," as anyone who has had their dog chase off a spook knows. Our dog has done this several times. Once the wind blew our door open (we assume it was the wind…) and our dog, barking, chased something around the room and back out the door as we sat with our mouths gaping. After shutting and locking the door, we gave him several treats. Sometimes it is better not to know.

From earliest times, dogs saw and protected us from things that go bump in the night including spirits, ghosts, and elemental spirits. In Shamanic traditions, dogs guard the shaman while they are soul traveling. Sometimes a shaman's robes were made of dog skin, indicating the magical connections between the two. The spirit dogs of the Welsh god Arawn, lord of the underworld, were said to chase the evil dead back to the underworld at the coming of fall. According to this tradition, the voices of the geese migrating were their cries. Maybe this is why our dog insists on furiously barking at every flock of honking geese flying overhead.

Unfortunately, we mostly need protecting from other humans. This is why we have a Beware of Dog sign on our door, though standard poodles are just not that scary, they can certainly bark. People in the ancient world would see our black dog as a fearsome protector and a possible representative of the protector of travelers, the Goddess Hecate, or of the hunting moon goddess Artemis, or even the Mesopotamian goddess Belit-ili. All of these goddesses protected through their dog spirits, maybe this is why guard dogs developed a serious spiritual reputation over the ages.

Though often they were black dogs, like Hecate's dogs, some protective dogs were different. Baby Zeus was protected by a special divine dog named Kyon Khryseos or "golden dog," which was given to him by the goddess Rhea. Zeus grew up to become king of the gods, so that dog was obviously great at his job.

Once we had a con man come to the door and harass us until our loyal dog drove him away. Our beloved furry protector got all the treats he wanted that day.

No matter what we are doing, where we live, and who we are, our dogs love and protect us from the seen and unseen worlds, this we know. This is one of their primal tasks, and they take it very seriously, thank goodness.

Spells, Meditations & Charms

Charm to Keep Away Dangerous Dogs

Dog power is kind and loving and healing, but it is also martial, defensive, and aggressive when it needs to be. Dogs *do* bite, after all, and our canines all have sharp canines. Not all dogs are nice, just like people. This is a charm to keep dangerous dogs away from you and from your dog as well.

You will need:

+ A small square of cloth that is red, maybe 5" by 5"
+ Some black thread or cord
+ Some dried hot peppers,
+ A small nail
+ A bit of dirt collected from a dog park or a place where many dogs go
+ A small cigar
+ A lighter or matches

Go to a quiet path that goes four ways at midday with your dog. Walk down each of the paths a few yards with your dog, saying:

Ashe, ashe, ashe, Ogu,*
Bring me power and protection.

At the point where all four paths meet place all the items in the cloth except the lighter, the cigar, and a pinch of the pepper.

Tie the ends of the cloth together to create a sachet. Sprinkle some pepper on the ground and on the packet, light the cigar, blow smoke in the circle to the four directions and on the packet five times and say:

Legba, Elegua, Exu,*
Help me now, protect me true,
From hunting dogs, war dogs, and crazy dogs, too.
Legba, Elegua, Exu,
Help me know, protect me true.
Ashe, ashe, ashe.
I thank you!

Blow up more smoke and leave. Keep the sachet with you, hang it by your door, or give it to a friend. If threatened by a dog, grab it and repeat the charm.

* Translation (Haitian Creole—roots in various
African Languages): Ashe = Hail or Praise! ; Ogu =
Afro-Caribbean Spirit associated with martial powers;
Legba (Vodou), Elegua (Santeria), Exu (Candoble) =
Guardians/Spirits of the Crossroads.

Guard Dog Spell

Your dog partner just wants to know what you want to do and how you want it done. So, if you want a guard dog, this spell will deeply imprint this desire within your furry friend.

You will need:
+ A small piece of paper and a red pen
+ A calm home
+ Dog treats
+ Matches

Before beginning, with very short, simple sentences, write the five things you want your dog to do, like: "Guard the house at night" or "Protect us when we are out."

When ready, center yourself and hold the paper, telling your dog how good it is and saying you have something to show it.

Read the five sentences to your dog in a clear, calm voice. Now take the treats and lead your dog to the front door, saying:

> *You are Fu Shi,*
> *The great lion-dog.*
> *Protect and defend,*
> *Hu.**

Give your dog a treat. Next, take your dog to the rear door (or back of the apartment), and say:

You are Cerberus,
The three-headed dark guardian.
Protect and defend,
Hu.

Give your dog a treat. Go to the right side of the house and say:

You are Cu Sith,
The giant green fey forest dog
Who sees and knows all.
Protect and defend us,
Hu.

Give your dog a treat. Go to the left side of the house and say:

You are Anubis; Anpu,
The jackal who knows all ways.
Guard every path and door,
Protect and defend,
Hu.

Give your dog a treat. Go to the center of the home, sit with your dog and say:

You are the dog of Odin, Artemis, and Herne.
You are the wolf and fox and dingo spirit.
Protect and defend,
Hu.

Give your dog a treat. Burn the paper and scatter the ashes around the outside of your home. Now, go play with your awesome dog. If it pees near your home, it is renewing its territory protection vows.

Translation (Egyptian): Hu = Power word—first word of Creation; let it be!

Dog Spirit Home Protection Charm

There is an ancient tradition of dog charms protecting one's home and this spell reenacts this in a more modern context. It is unlikely that you can dig up the entryway of your home to bury something anymore, but we can adapt. If you can find a place to put this charm near your door or bury it next to your front door, you will add a layer of magical protection to your abode thanks to the Dog Spirit. This is based upon a real ancient Mesopotamian spell.

You will need:
+ A small amount of bee's wax
+ A bit of your dog's hair
+ A pin or a ritual dagger with a small point

On the full moon, at noon on a sunny day, in a sacred place of your choosing knead the wax and the dog hair together. Focusing your will, chant:

Sun mother, Arinna,
Moon man, Kashku,
Sun and moon
Empower you.
*Kalbum.**

When done, mold the wax into a small dog. It doesn't have to be perfect. Using the pin or knifepoint, take the little wax dog and in it carve a small moon on one side, a small sun on the other, and your name along the top. Then say:

You are a powerful dog
Of the table of the royal pair.
Just as by day you protect this home,
So too let no evil come by night.
Ari-n-na.
Ka-sh-ku.
Kalbum.
Let it be so.

Now bury the charm near your front door or place it by your door and say:

You are banished by the three.
Come too close and you must flee.
By this charm so shall it be.

Ari-n-na.
Ka-sh-ku.
Kalbum.
Let it be so.

Get your dog to bark and, after it barks, say:

Tread not here.
Tread not there.
Touch nothing.
All beware.
Kalbum.

Your spirit dog will protect you even when your real dog is out for a walk.

* Translation (Akkadian): Kalbum = Dog. Arinna is the Hittite goddess of the sun, and Kashku is the god of the moon.

Spell to Protect Your Dog from Thieves & Harm

One thing scary about loving your pooch so much is the idea that some truly evil, dastardly thief might take your beloved furry friend. Though it doesn't pay to be paranoid, it also never pays to be slack. This is where magic fits the bill. Worried about nameless dognappers? Do this spell to repel all dog thieves. And don't leave your pal unattended (or in a hot car)!

You will need:

- A dark purple permanent marker pen
- The dog's collar
- Some lavender oil

On a Wednesday morning, open your window to the breeze and place all three items on the windowsill. Raise your hands and say:

> Hermanubis lightfoot,
> Dog god of the fleet,
> Protect my friend
> On path and street.
> Thieves and dog
> Never meet.
> Chaire amyntor.*

On the inside of the collar, draw the following sign with your purple pen: ⸶

After that, put some of the lavender oil on the symbol. Then hold it up to the sky and say:

> Chaire amyntor.
> Chaire Hermanubis.*
> So may it be
> Forever more.

Put the collar on the dog, then rub a very little bit of the oil on your dog. See your dog protected by blue light. No one is going to mess with your cosmically charged pooch.

> *Translation (Greek): Chaire amyntor = We welcome you, Defender!; Chaire Hermanubis = We greet you, Hermanubis (the dog-headed)!*

Help Prevent a Lost Dog Spell

If you have a flighty dog or one that wanders often, or even if you are just worried about your dog straying, this spell is for you.

You will need:
+ A small silver bowl with natural sea salt
+ Spring water in a silver bowl
+ An arrow
+ A rattle
+ A yellow or "golden apple"

When the new crescent moon first appears, take your dog to the front door and stop on your stoop, just as you walk out of the house.

Take the salt in your hand and salute the crescent moon, saying:

By the light of Artemis bow,
This you now shall see and know.
If you wander off and then,
She shall guide you back again.

Sprinkle a small pinch of salt on your dog's tail, head, and four paws. Taste the salt and give your dog a tiny bit to taste as well. Sprinkle water on both of you, drink some, and give the rest to your dog to drink.

Pick up the arrow in one hand and the rattle in the other. Slowly circle your dog and visualize it shielded and protected while shaking the rattle and holding the arrow up above your head, saying:

> Protect, empower, and heal!
> With this chant
> I make it real.
> Eulogia bios.*

Now take a bite out of the apple and let your dog smell it. Remove the seeds as you chant:

> Seed to beast,
> Seed to beast,
> I am the large
> And the very least.

Take the seeds and put them in the bowl that had water in it. Hold the bowl up to the moon. Sprinkle the water and the seeds around your doorway and say:

> You are mine,
> And I am yours.

This is your home
This spell will ensure.

Once finished, raise your hands to the moon in thanks. To the goddess Artemis say three times:

Thelema. Agape. IAO.

Now take your dog inside and lock the door.

* *Translation (Greek): Eulogia bios = Divine Praise for Life; Thelema. Agape. IAO. = Will. Love. Healing/ Light.*

Take Your Dog to Work for Protection & Help Charm

All would be perfect in the world if you could bring your beloved dog to work. In some workplaces it is the norm to bring your dog to spend the day with you at your office. This is a charm that will make even coworkers at the office who don't own a dog welcome your tail-wagging friend. Your dog can also protect you from office trolls and negative people, such is the power of its positive energy. If a welcoming work environment for you and your dog is what you desire, then try this charm to influence policies at work. This little bit of magic should soon allow your furry companion to join you at your work site.

You will need:

- Picture of your dog printed from your work computer
- Your business card
- Stapler/staples
- A black pen
- A blue candle
- A brown candle
- Matches or lighter
- A sheet of your company's stationary
- An office envelope with the return address for the name of your company
- A stamp

When the moon is waxing take your business card and staple it to the photo of your dog. Now take the pen and draw the image of the company's logo or name on the back of the photo and say:

(Name of your dog) *must come everywhere with me,*
Especially to (name of company or place).
At work or at play,
(Name of your dog) *and I want to stay*
Together all day!

Light the blue candle and say three times:

Tui.*

Light the brown candle and say three times:

Ken.*

Now say three times:

Tui ken.*

Now say three times:

Hsien.*
So may it be.

Draw on the sheet of stationary this I Ching Hexagram: ䷞

This I Ching Hexagram means "influence, success, and perseverance," and it will help you to further your goals.

Now fold the piece of stationary and place the photo and card inside it. Take the envelope and address it to yourself at work, all the time visualizing your dog snoozing under your desk. Lick the envelope closed and visualize your dog giving you a kiss, place the stamp on it, and drop the envelope in the mail.

When your charm arrives back to you, tape it under your desk directly over where your dog will lay. Now wait for the memo from your job announcing the change in the company policy, that now it will allow dogs at your company. Now you both will be together at work and play all day.

* *Translation (Chinese): Tui = Lake; Ken = Mountain (both are trigrams); joined together they make the I Ching Hexagram Hsien = Influence.*

Chapter Six

Dog Guide Magic

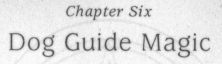

Tracking & Finding Valuables, People & Your Dog

Have you ever gotten lost in a familiar place? One time we got completely turned around and lost inside a ninety-acre park, and we kept emerging at unfamiliar spots and it was getting dark. Finally, Thor had enough and, yelping at us, took the lead. Leash pulled tight, he unerringly guided us through the maze of trees right to our car. We were amazed, but why were we?

Dog Guides

Eons ago our dog friends guided us while we were tracking mastodons and protected us from sabre tooth tigers lurking at the edge of our fires. From long ago until today, dogs have been tracking our game and flushing out prey and so humans have kept hunger at bay with the help of our furry friends. The seemingly miraculous ability of dogs to smell and follow scents we cannot has saved many from the perils of woodland trails or battlefields or hunger. And, when we take our last journey, it is said that dogs will help us make it through the gate of death safely to the afterlife.

A great and lasting mythic example of dog magic guiding is the Wild Hunt. Sounds like fun, doesn't it? Not if you lived in Europe hundreds of years ago. In the Wild Hunt, the old ancient Powers roamed the night skies led by packs of spirit dogs, hunting demons, spirits, and, sometimes, unlucky people who were out late at night. This myth was huge in Celtic, Nordic, and Germanic countries. Depending on the myths, the Wild Hunt is led by faerie or the honored dead, by divine heroes like Nuada or King Arthur, by a wild god like Odin or Herne, or by a powerful goddess like Holle or Holda, depending on who tells the tale. This howling hunt sweeps through the spirit and physical worlds at night as fall turns to winter. Interestingly enough, a similar myth is described in India, where a fearsome aspect of Bhairav Shiva leads a spirit hunt with his sacred dogs.

The origin of this Wild Hunt is likely in ritual enactments of the divine hunt, reflecting the era when tribes survived or perished depending on success in the hunt for game. It is traditionally warned that whomever witnesses the Wild Hunt must join in.

Many hunting gods called upon their divine dogs in helping guide them and track prey. In Greek myths, examples include Artemis, the hero Orion, and even Hercules. In Greece, we never saw a statue of Artemis without her hounds. Around the globe we find other hunter gods accompanied by hunting dogs, such as the Hittite god Rundas, the Fon god Gu, or the Yoruban god Ogun.

Just as we are sure to get lost in the woods at times, so too do our faculties decline as we get older. A sad truth more readily apparent every year. We will need help with more mundane guidance, and dogs and dog spirits are there to help us, just as they assisted the great heroes of legend. A hero-dog helped Hercules in his final days, and the hound Cavall guided King Arthur on many adventures, even to his last. We know a sight-impaired friend who depends on her guide dog just as in ancient times a famous dog guided blind Homer from city to city. Today we see the indomitable spirit of dog heroes guiding and protecting not only the blind but also those with physical or cognitive afflictions. Where would we be without the protection and guidance our beloved dogs have provided these many thousands of years?

Spells, Meditations & Charms

Meditation with Your Dog to Find Lost Items

"Now where did I put that?" or "I just saw it a minute ago…" is a constant refrain for many of us. No matter where you look, you can never find what you are looking for, yet you live with the perfect tracker: your dog. Dogs have been used for finding missing people, places, or things stretching back thousands of years. We would literally be lost without their constant ability to track down things you ask them to find. Once on the search, dogs are tenacious and unrelenting. Dogs are normally guided by the smell to find what you are looking for. If you are searching for something missing you can do this simple mediation that will help both of you in a successful hunt in finding whatever you are looking for.

You will need:

+ Sage
+ Matches or a lighter

Since you looked everywhere for what is missing you will need clarity and focus for success in the hunt. Light the sage and smudge the area where you last remember seeing your object. Now have your dog sit in front of you so it can lead the way to what is missing. Pet its nose, and as you close your eyes both of you relax. Wait until the feeling of frustration from not finding what you are looking for is gone, and say:

> *Power of my dog,*
> *Come to me.*
> *May I see the way you see,*
> *May I smell what you smell,*
> *And seek* (say object missing here).
> *May all go well.*

Now, in your mind's eye, visualize what you are looking for and where you last saw it. Now tell your dog what you need help locating. All the while keep stroking your dog's head and snout, visualizing it searching to find what you want to get back. Place your hand over your eyes then your dog's eyes, do the same on your ears and then your dog's ears, then on your nose and then your dog's nose. Say:

Old man Coyote
Old man Coytl
Old man Sinawava
Old man Tlapus
Old man Yelis*

Mediate on your dog getting up and finding what you want. A deep connection between the both of you to find the same thing at the same time will help with a successful hunt. Your dog will pick up from your thoughts what you are looking for during this meditation. When you are finished with your mediation whisper what you want your dog to find in its ear and give it the instruction to help you search. Say:

Coyote spirit,
May I find
What I See
With Coyote Mind.
May my dog fill me with coyotl scent.
So may it be.

Together you should both find what you are looking in no time at all.

* Translation (Various): All different Native American tribal names for Grandfather Coyote.

Spell to Make Your Dog a Top Guide Dog

We all need help in life, and that is the truth. Our dogs guide us every day in so many ways, and some people with disabilities need their dogs to be extra special guide dogs. Whether you are working with assistance dogs or seeing-eye dogs or simply want your dog to be a sharp guide or focused hunting hound, this spell may help awaken the "inner guide" in your loyal dog.

You will need:
+ A small piece of amber
+ A little honey
+ A sunny day

Take your dog to a nice, sunny, natural place, or a path where another path intersects in a park. When you are both relaxed, maybe after a walk, stand in the sunlight, hold up the amber to the sun, and say:

> O shining Dog Spirit
> Of Apollo Cunomaglus,
> Great sun dog
> Kyon Khryseos,
> Lailaps, brilliant divine dog of Orion,
> Open our eyes, hearts, and minds.
> Sol Invictus.*

Close your eyes and touch the warm amber to your left and right eyes, saying each time:

Sol Invictus.

Do the same with your dog's eyes, making sure they are closed.

Take the honey, hold it up to the east, south, west, and north. At each corner, say:

As the sun guides the day
You will guide me
Come what may.
To each direction
You will know
How to guide me.
Make it so.

Eat some of the honey. Then feed some to your dog and offer it to the sun. When done, hug your dog, feel the solar energy fill you both, and open your awareness. Raise your arms and say:

Sol Invictus.
*Lux Fiat.**

Ask your dog to guide you true and maybe give it a treat. Go and have fun. Keep the amber as a solar talisman.

* *Translation (Latin): Sol Invictus = Victory to the sun;*
Lux Fiat = Let there be light.

Spirit Dog Tracker Spell

Spirit Dogs are dogs that you owned in the past, visions you have of dogs, or dogs that you don't know yet but whom in the future you will connect to. Having a spirit dog to guide you, protect you, or give you spiritual advice are just a few of the ways that you can use your spirit dog. These dogs provide very powerful "dog medicine" and will come at your call when you are in need. They are dog companions working to please you, even if they are invisible to others. Spirit dogs will help you become more psychic and more in touch and attuned to the spiritual world. You might conjure a spirit dog to help find whatever notion you are seeking, be it health, love, or anything else. This spell will help you connect with a dog spirit to track and lead the way on any successful search.

You will need:
+ A white candle
+ Matches
+ A dog whistle
+ Paper
+ A dog treat

At midnight, light the candle and stare into it, visualizing the dog spirit that you want to conjure. As you do this, say its name or the type of dog spirit three times, then followed with what you want it to find three times. Place the dog whistle next to the candle. As you stare into the candle, visualize your spirit dog descending and floating above the candle flame. Write on the paper what you wish to find in your life and have your dog spirit track, fetch, and retrieve it for you.

Now say:

Spirit dog of vision,
Spirit dog of sight,
Bring to me what I desire
By day or night.
Spirit dog of vision,
Spirit dog of sight,
Come when I whistle
By day or night.
Spirit dog of vision,
Spirit dog of sight,
I conjure you this day
Come to me this night.
*Spiritus Grimm Conjurare Est.**

Now roll up the piece of paper and burn it, saying:

Spirit dog guide me
Bring me to my need
Lead to my ambitions.
Let my will be freed.
*Spiritus Grimm Conjurare Est. Fiat.**

Blow the whistle and "see" the spirit dog race off to grant your desire. Keep the whistle. Blow it and repeat the invocation any time you want to conjure your dog spirit to guide some good luck to you or help for tracking or guiding on a new quest.

Translation (Latin): Spiritus Grimm Conjurare Est = I conjure now the dog spirit of this place; Fiat = It is done.

Spell to Find a Lost Dog

Almost nothing is more traumatic than having your dog vanish. Dogs get lost like people do, and sometimes they become hurt or confused. This is heartbreaking. Prevention is always best; making sure you have clear tags and maybe even a microchip on your dog is the best step you can take if you worry your pet might get lost. Both can help recover a dog, but not always. If your dog is lost, this spell might help. Good luck.

You will need:
+ "Lost dog" flyers you plan to put up in the neighborhood
+ A silver or light blue pencil or pen
+ Some lavender or some form of incense ascribed to the planet Mercury
+ A lighter or matches

Before you print up the flyers, find a time for calmness. Open your front door and sit in front of it, looking out. Do this at a time you will not be disturbed. Have the flyers and a pen before you. Light the incense and say:

Io Evoe Hermes.*
Fleet of foot, lord of roads and ways,
Seek and help my dog return to me
On all the nights and all the days.
Io Evoe Hermes—so may it be.

Wave the flyers through the smoke three times; see them filled with silvery-blue energy of Hermes/Mercury.

On the back of each flyer, draw the planetary symbol of mercury ☿ with an eye in the center. When finished, go out and put these flyers up. Good luck finding your furry friend.

* Translation (Greek): Io Evoe Hermes = Yea/Hail Hermes.

Spell to Find the Perfect Dog Sitter or Walker

Time to take a trip or go to work and you can't take your beloved pooch with you? Leaving your dog behind in someone else's care is often a little nerve-racking. Not being home with your dog is hard on it, too. In times like these, you need the perfect dog sitter or walker. Someone not only great with your dog, but someone you feel comfortable with, too. How do you find a dog sitter or walker who is reliable, caring, and great with your dog? You will need a little magic, like this spell, to find and fetch the perfect dog sitter.

You will need:
+ Paper
+ Pen
+ Blue candle
+ Matches

Write everything you want from a dog walker or sitter on the paper then say:

> *We need a helper who is loving and kind,*
> *Who will take care of you all of the time.*
> *Holda, Holle, dog mother dear,*
> *Bring us a dog helper without any fear.*
> *Dagaz.**

Lightly carve the Dagaz rune ᛞ into the candle with your fingernail. Light the candle and say:

> *Dagaz, Dagaz, Dagaz.*
> *I won't be gone long.*
> *I will not flee.*
> *I will find you the*
> *Perfect sitter to be.*

Now burn the paper and as the paper burns, say:

A good match the sitter will be,
Like a pack member, an extended family.
We will miss you this is true,
But time will pass quickly
Till returned home to you.
Dagaz, Dagaz, Dagaz.

Let the candle burn out completely, then look for a good dog sitter or dog walker, the right one will appear.

* Translation (Norse): Holle and Holda are ancient wild Earth Goddess names; Dagaz is a Rune—meaning Light, Protection, Divinity.

Finding the Perfect Home for You & Your Dog Spell

Time to move? Finding a home that works for you and your dog can take some effort. Not only does it need to fit your requirements, it needs to fit your dog's needs, too. If you are looking for a new apartment, it should be near a park where you both can go on walks together. If you are looking for a house, you should try to get a fenced in yard. Your needs are different from your dog's needs, so you both need to find a place to live in harmony. Finding the perfect home for both of you should be a little easier with this spell.

You will need:

+ A piece of paper
+ A pen
+ A map of the general area you want to move to
+ A stick of sandalwood incense
+ Matches or lighter
+ A white flower
+ A small cup of milk

Perform this spell on a full moon. Take the piece of paper and make columns for you and your dog and any others moving with you. At the top of each column, write the name of your dog, your name, and any other family member's names. Under each name write what they desire in a new home. Now go through the list and cross off any duplicate items. Take the map and write on the back all the items you share in common.

Now draw a big round moon on the map. Fold up the map and light the incense, waving it over the map, and say.

Om Sarama Devi,* dog goddess of the moon,
Send out your clever dogs,
Find us a home soon.
Adya sarama devata svaha*
Grant us this boon.

Place the incense where you normally burn it and let it burn out. Take the flower, hold it to your third eye, and then hold it to your dog's third eye. Put your hands together, look up at the moon, and offer the flower to it. Saying three times as you move your hand back and forth:

*Om Namaste Sarama Devi.**

Say one time:

Sarama-Ha.

Drink some of the milk and share it with your dog. When the incense finishes burning out take your map and go off to find your new home. When you find it, offer incense and a white flower there to Sarama Devi, and thank her.

* *Translation (Sanskrit): Om Sarama Devi = We greet you, Sarama Goddess; Adya sarama devata svaha= Primal Sarama Goddess, we worship you, so be it!; Ha = roughly "let it happen."*

Chapter Seven

Dog Fidelity

Invoking Devotion, Loyalty & Obedience with & for Your Dog

"Loyal as a dog" is a favorite idiom worldwide, and why not? There is always a media story about a loyal dog finding its long-lost owners. Devotion knows no geographical limits it seems.

Once when we were home, our puppy somehow slipped out of the house and into the neighbor's yard. In a panic, we looked everywhere until we heard a howl at the front door, where he patiently waited to get back in. "Where have you been?" he seemed to say, and he has remained our shadow ever since.

Loyal & Devoted Dogs

From earliest times, dogs have been a symbol of loyalty and fidelity across the globe. My husband grew up with a big dog named Fido and we laughed together about that silly name until we started writing this book. Why? Because Fido originates from the Latin *Fidus*, meaning "trust" or "faithful," and dogs, like the Marines, are "always faithful" or *semper fi*.

In Roman art, dogs appeared as the main symbol of loyalty, trust, and faithfulness, often depicted on tombs at the feet of their masters. Women are traditionally depicted in sculpture and paintings from ancient days through the modern romantic period alongside dogs, indicating faithfulness and fidelity. Even the allegorical image of the classical Grace "Fidelity" depicts her with a dog. History, myth, and art tell stories of dog's undying loyalty.

Mythically, Zeus's dog loyally protected him from dangers as a helpless baby. Argo, the dog of Odysseus, was the only one to recognize Odysseus upon his return to Ithaca twenty years later, becoming a favorite classical Greek symbol for undying devotion. In ancient Rome, the historian Pliny wrote of a dog refusing to leave the side of his deathly ill master, Titus Labienus.

In the Zoroastrian holy book *The Avesta*, dogs appear as symbols of "vigilance and loyalty" and are never to be mistreated and always to be shown love and affection. Even a dog's gaze possesses spiritual power and *Ihtiram-i sag*, a phrase commonly used in this religion meaning "respect for the loyal dog."

Traveling in the United Kingdom, you can't help but noticing the British are dog crazy, with none extolling the loyalty of dogs more that the corgi-loving Queen herself. This persists in Celtic countries from the earliest times, where fidelity became linked with the word for dog, CU, a synonym for loyalty. The great hero Cú Chulainn (Hound of Culann) was bestowed this name in honor of his faithfulness. Later on, King Arthur, in tales sometimes referred to as "great dog," owned a semi-divine dog hero named Cavall (Cavell, Cafell, Cabal, or Caball). This mighty being hunted with King Arthur, and they had great adventures and mythic hunts. He saved the king from many perils and so was honored as a symbol of loyalty. Many special places in Wales and elsewhere in the United Kingdom are named after him, honoring this dog hero to this day.

In China, we find another super loyal mythic dog accompanying the legendary hero Erlang, a character in *Journey to the West*, the epic of the Monkey King. In this mythic novel, Erlang's feisty hound comes to the rescue and defeats the monster. This popular tale epitomizes the loyalty of dogs in China and Tibet. When we traveled in China in the early 1990s, we often noticed that gods and emperors (even Chairman Mao) were depicted in paintings and sculpture with their hounds, thus, we were told, lending themselves qualities of loyalty and trustworthiness, whether true or not.

In the popular Chinese Zodiac, "dog people" are intensely devoted and loyal. In Tibetan Buddhism, one myth claims the lion-dog protected the Buddha and his teachings, becoming a symbol of diligence, devotion, and loyalty.

In India, the dog's loyalty and devotion is honored during the five-day Tihar Festival, where all dogs are fed, decked in flowers, and revered as objects of devotion. The Hindu god-saint Datta-treya is always shown surrounded by dogs, said to represent his devotees, being symbols of loyalty and religious devotion to the Guru.

As Christianity spread, the dog became a favorite symbol of devotion to God and the loyalty of true converts. Several Christian saints were accompanied by loyal dogs. Saint Roch, who lived in the early fourteenth century in France, is a patron saint of dogs because of the following story. Saint Roch became very ill while performing good works among the sick, and he went to the forest to die. In the forest, a loyal dog befriended the sick man and brought him food. Under the dog's care Saint Roch recovered and forever gave honor to the divine dog intervention. In some places, his feast day is celebrated as the "feast of all dogs," where their devotion and loyalty is honored. We trust that every dog there gets lots of good dog treats that day.

From time immemorial, dogs are described as "man's best friend." What could possibly be a better symbol of devotion, loyalty, and fidelity? Just ask our dog, who never leaves our side and often sits at our feet as we write books like this.

Spells, Meditations & Charms

Obey Me Behavior Spell

Good Dog. How you long to say those words. But instead, you may find the limits of your patience tried. It is for both you and your dog's well-being that your dog behaves. Do not feel your dog is defiant or antiauthority, some dogs are just a little more stubborn than others and need more help learning the rules.

If nothing seems to work getting your dog to obey you, first make sure you both have a clear understanding of what is expected from each other. Having an obedient dog that does not do destructive doggie things makes a more peaceful life for both of you. Good dog manners make your dog a good citizen. Whatever your dog does that you find undesirable, the unwanted behavior is changeable with a little dog training and this spell.

You will need:
+ A red candle
+ Pens; one red, one black
+ A black candle
+ Matches
+ Your dog's collar and leash
+ Dog toys
+ Treats

Take the red candle and, using the red pen, write on the candle what you want your dog to do. Now pick up the black candle and write with the black pen what you want your dog not to do. Light the black candle and say:

> *You need to behave.*
> *You need to mind.*
> *Do what you are told*
> *All of the time.*

Now draw a downward pointing triangle ▽ over what you wrote on the black candle. Say:

> *This is what we need to do:*
> *We both need to work together*
> *And respect one another too.*
> *By Geki and Freki; make it true.*
> *Galderbyorg.**

Let the black candle burn.

Place the dog collar, leash, dog toys, and treats near the red and black candles. Light the red candle, take the red pen, and draw a triangle pointing up △, and say:

> *You will listen.*
> *You will behave.*
> *Because I guide you,*
> *Now be this way.*
> *So may it be*
> *By Feya and Frey.*
> *Galderbyorg.*

Say:

> *With this oath*
> *This spell is done.*
> *This spell is cast*
> *Our wills are one.*

Give your dog the treats. Place both candles together and let them burn down. Be ready for a new, more compliant dog.

* *Translation (Norse): Galderbyorg = You are protected/ empowered by this spell.*

No Begging Spell

Oh, how tempting people food is for your dog! Your dog begging for your scraps is completely natural. Dogs and people entered a pact together thousands of years ago: dogs keep guard and bark if danger appears and in return they are fed scraps. Now dogs can do both; they can still guard you, but instead of eating your food they can eat their own dog food. You might find it tempting to indulge your dog at the table, especially with your furry friend begging for just a morsel. Having a dog content to watch you eat and not ask for handouts is possible, just try this spell to make peace at the table.

You will need:
+ A plate you eat off of
+ Your dog's bowl
+ Nontoxic erasable black marker or crayon
+ Dog food
+ Some of your food

Hold your plate and your dog's bowl and say to your dog:

> By Odin's wolves,
> Here is my spell:
> Though separate dishes
> Together we dwell.

Take the marker and respectfully draw this hagaz rune ᚺ on the bottom of your plate. As you draw this rune, speak these words:

> Wolf and man,
> We have an ancient pact, you and me.
> You guard me and I feed thee.
> This is your food and this is mine.
> Do not beg now or for the rest of time.
> Hagaz.*

Now draw the same rune on your dog's bowl and say:

> By Odin's wolves,
> This food I give
> To my loyal wolf
> So he might live.
> This food is yours.
> This food is good.
> Eat only this
> As you should.
> Hagaz.

Now dish up your meal on your plate and feed your dog its meal in the bowl. Before eating, say:

> *We are hungry,*
> *You and me.*
> *We do not share,*
> *My food let be.*
> *My food is mine.*
> *Your food is yours.*
> *Now we will eat*
> *In each other's company.*
> *Hagaz.*

Anytime your dog begs for food hold up your hand then point to your dog's bowl and say:

> *Hagaz.*

Now sit down and eat.

> ** Translation (Norse): Hagaz is a rune; here it means a sudden shift, change, or action—a correction in behavior.*

Mindful Loyalty Spell

Owning a dog is a great responsibility and one you must keep a focus on in your busy life. Juggling work, play, and errands makes it easy to forget your dog in the hustle. To keep yourself reminded and focused on your quiet, loyal companion and forge a deeper bond with your dog, try this spell. Plus, it is great fun.

You will need:
+ Some newspaper
+ Self-hardening modeling clay (plaster or clay if you are more crafty)
+ A little fur from your dog
+ A few strands of your hair
+ A sprig of rosemary

In the morning, place the newspaper on the ground and lay out the items facing east. Make sure your dog is with you. You can be at home or outside. Face the rising sun and say:

> By Cavall, the loyal Dog Spirit of King Arthur,
> By the hound of Cú Chulainn the divine,
> By Gwydion, the leader of the hunt,
> I am yours and you are mine.

Flatten out the molding clay to about hands-breadth. Press your hand into it. Then gently take your dog's paw and press it into the clay so a good impression is made.

Take a little of your dog's fur and a couple strands of your hair and say:

> My hounds of heroes,
> My hands of spirit,

We are loyal together forever.
Loyal to the end
By the power of Cavall.
So be it.

Press your hair and your dog's fur into the clay. Finally, press the small sprig of rosemary into the center of it, saying:

An làmb a bheir, 's i a gheibh*

When done, shake your dog's paw, hug (and maybe kiss) your dog. Make a small hole near the top of the paw print piece and, when it finishes drying, hang it up as a charm to be forever true to each other.

* *Translation (Gaelic): An làmb a bheir, 's i a gheibh =* *"the hand that gives is the hand that gets."*

Painless Piddle & Poop Training Charm

A new pup is scared and needs lots of hugging and support. Yet, there is something that we want that puppy to do ASAP, and that is to pee on the paper you have out. Yet, you don't want to traumatize or even speak harshly to the cute little thing, how could you? This spell, along with some gentle guidance, will get that pup headed in the right piddle direction.

You will need:

+ Some cider vinegar
+ Some common grass
+ A small bowl
+ A small artist's paintbrush
+ Some newspaper to put down

At sunset, put the vinegar and the grass in a small bowl. Let it sit for several hours. When ready to cast the spell, lay out the paper on the floor near the pup. Take the bowl of vinegar and grass in one hand and the paintbrush in the other, and walk around the paper three times, saying:

Here's your space
To poop and pee.
Here your place,
Baj* let it be.

Now, dip the paintbrush into the grassy vinegar and paint a large, sweeping counterclockwise spiral in the center of the paper on the floor saying *Baj* several times.

If your dog pees or poops somewhere else clean him up and bring him back to the paper and sit him in the spiral. Now say:

No, puppy, no,
This will not do.
This is the place that you pee and poo.
The spell of bad

Come what may,
Pee and poop here
You must obey.
Baj.

Your pup will get the idea faster than you can say "Not on my oriental rug."

*   * Translation: Baj = a minor elemental spirit of pee and*
*   poop of uncertain origin.*

Trust Me & Leave It Spell

Dogs prefer obeying and doing what they are told. Even the most obedient dog will not be able resist a temptation like smelly, dead things to roll in or perhaps another animal catches its interest. This spell will help your dog trust and obey you even in the most tempting situations.

You will need:
+ A dried oak leaf
+ A plate
+ A red strip of ribbon or fabric (natural material about six inches long)
+ A permanent green marker
+ Matches or a lighter

On a Tuesday at first light, crumble the oak leaf on the plate and light it. As it smokes, pass the red ribbon through the smoke ten times, saying:

> *Strong as an oak,*
> *Tough as wood.*
> *Fearless and strong,*
> *Do what you should.*
> *Fortis.**

With the green marker, carefully draw the following Theban letters on the red band, ꝏ Ʊ ꞁ ꝝ saying:

> *Fortis, Fortis,*
> *Strong and fast,*
> *By this charm*
> *Spirit ever last.*

Light the leaf again, pass the band through the smoke three more times, and repeat the same verse. Then say:

> *(Your dog's name),*
> *You need to trust and mind.*
> *Do not let your urges blind.*
> *Do not do without command*
> *At home or roaming on the land.*
> *Leave it and walk away.*

Be a good dog and trust, obey.
Like I know you can do.
*Canem obedire, fiat.**

Scatter the rest of the ashes and leaf bits outside when it finishes burning out.

Wrap the ribbon around your dog's collar and say:

*Minerva dea, fiat.**

If your dog just does not want to leave well enough alone, then anytime this situation appears, say.

Fortis.

* *Translation (Latin): Fortis = Strength; Canem obedire, fiat = Dog, obey me, so may it be; Minerva dea, fiat = By the goddess Minerva, so may it be.*

What Do You Need? Meditation

Sometimes your dog does crazy-looking things. Some behaviors become a nuisance and may seem illogical or problematic. Often your dog is doing such things because of reasons they cannot communicate. Such behaviors, while irritating, are a cry for understanding. This meditation will help get to the root of these problems.

You will need:

+ A rock with a natural hole in it
+ String
+ A white candle
+ Matches or lighter
+ Some dried sage
+ A blue candle

Wait until your dog does the strange behavior, chewing up the couch or whatever it is. Instead of disciplining your dog, sit quietly with it and breathe deeply until you are both calm. Take the rock and put the string through it. Rocks with holes are very magical, especially if you found one near water. Hold the rock in your right hand and swing it gently in front of you both until the rock stops swinging on its own. Now light the white candle, look into the flame, and say:

> *I know you are good,*
> *I know you are well,*
> *I know that you need something*
> *That I cannot tell.*
> *Coyalto.**

Take the sage and crush some in your hand, inhaling the scent. Have your dog smell it a bit too. Rub a bit on your third eye and on your dog's head, gently.

Light the blue candle and say:

> *Reveal to me*
> *What you need.*
> *Show me a sign*
> *So we both can rest easily.*
> *Coyalto.*

Place your hand around or on your dog. Close your eyes and ask your dog, mentally, why are you doing this? What do you need? Now say:

> *Old Man Coyote,*
> *I call to thee.*
> *By the wisdom way*
> *Help me see.*
> *Spirit of trickster*
> *And mischievous deeds,*
> *Coyalto spirit,*
> *Show me his needs.*

Open your mind to receive images and feelings from your dog. You will get clear images and ideas on what is going on and what your dog needs to stop these behaviors. Maybe your pal needs more attention. Maybe a calmer environment. Maybe they hate the smell of that chair. You will see.

When you are clear and done with the psychic meditation, hug your dog, affirm your love, and sprinkle the sage about you both. Then give your pup a treat.

* *Translation (Nahuatl): Coyalto = Coyote Spirit/God.*

Chapter Eight

Dog Omens
& Totems

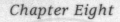

Your Spirit Dog Totems
& Dog Fortunetelling

Do you let your dog make important decisions? We do sometimes. For example, we were trying to decide which beach on the Washington coast to visit with our family. Our dog appeared quite attentive to our discussion of the pros and cons of several, so we asked him which one he wanted to visit. We read three of them aloud and he wagged his tail at number two. We did this three times; each time he picked the second beach. We asked him, "Are you sure?" He woofed. So, that is where we went. All places were new to him and to us, so it was a form of divination—and you know what? It was perfect for all of us.

Dog Magic, Totems & Omens

Dogs have been used for divination, magic, and paranormal exploration since they first started scaring phantoms away from Neanderthal campfires. For thousands of years, Dog Spirit and other divine canines have been invoked magically to heal, protect, and banish and to help develop psychic powers. It is therefore not surprising that shamans, witches, sorcerers, priests, priestesses, and magic makers throughout history used dog spirits, familiars, and totems to accomplish their magic. Even the great adept Agrippa and the dark sorcerer Faust had black dog familiars to help them conjure and see spirits.

My husband grew up in a large old house on the East Coast and he always talked about how the family dog Fido barked at things that weren't there, especially at one spot on their staircase. How many of you have had this experience? We know many who have. It seems our faithful dogs guard us from things that go bump in the night as well as burglars.

Dogs and dog images have often guarded temples, homes, and sacred places from demonic beings. Even today you will find dog statues at the entrance to mansions, though most have forgotten why they are there. In other countries, such as China where Foo Dogs guard in the same way, people still remember.

Dogs themselves can also protect us. The Parsee believe that dog breath will banish evil spirits or energies, probably because it is not so pleasant. The Parsee also use dogs as a medium for communicating with the dead.

Dogs can act as mediums. A number of shamanic cultures describe ageless traditions of human souls possessing dogs for the purpose of communication, divination, or sorcery.

Dogs were considered as particularly magical sacrifices in the past as well, poor things. During the hot dog days in ancient Rome, as pestilence threatened the populace, priests sacrificed dogs to the gods. A black dog in Greece and Rome was often offered to Hecate to ward off illness or for spells of protection or revenge. The Iroquois Native Americans long ago sacrificed a white dog at the New Year's ceremony so the dog sacrifice could bring all the prayers of the tribe to the attention of the Great Spirit.

In Mesoamerica, the Mayan, who venerated dogs, sacrificed a spotted dog to stop or avert a calamity such as earthquake or famine. Such ritually offered beings could intercede with the gods or offer a burst of powerful occult energy, though the practice seems barbaric today.

Today, symbolic dog charms replace the practice of actual sacrificial offerings. In Japan, a wooden dog "Emma" (a small wooden prayer plaque) is left at shrines to grant wishes, and *omamori* ("charms") of sumo dogs are sold at shrines and temples to keep a home or business safe. Foo lion-dogs and Inari foxes are placed in front of shrines, this is similar to dog statues found at the entrances of temples in ancient Babylon, Greece, and Rome. At many of these shrines, the dog was often called the "magical protector" of the Goddess and those who worshipped her. We have a dog omamori we got at a Japanese Shinto shrine hanging from the mirror of our car with the dog looking out the window, magically keeping dumb drivers away. It is funny to see our dog leaning his head out the window in a similar fashion.

In several cultures, small dog charms are buried under entryways or carried on one's person. In Taoist magic, straw dog charms catch, filter, and hold curses so they can be burned and eliminated.

Dogs also possess magical power as sacred ancestors or totem spirits in various cultures. To those who practice Norse magic (Seidr) the wolf is a powerful totem and spiritual force. Asatru followers even today use this power in their work. Amongst the Vikings and similar cultures, magical possession by this power conferred great strength, bravery, and fierceness along with resistance to pain and injury. This is likely how some of the werewolf legends arose. Shamans encountered wolf or dog spirits regularly from early on when exploring the spirit world. Another example is the ancient Irish dog bards ("Cainte") whose songs of satire could curse people. Even in today's modern armies, so-called "dog soldiers" are some of the fiercest and most loyal fighters.

Many deities, especially goddesses including Belit-ili, Gula, and Hecate, have appeared in the form of dogs in visions and dreams to give blessing and messages to their devotees. Dog spirits can also manifest as natural forces, like in the Philippines where the dog god Kimat represents lightning that can "bite" things. Calling upon these gods can prevent lightning damage.

Ever heard of "hair of the dog that bit you?" Though now it means to drink a bit to lessen a hangover, it references an old tradition of sympathetic dog magic. Having dog or wolf hair, especially from a dog that bit you, was an ancient protective measure against rabies.

It saddens me to describe certain practices and one of these is the tradition of using parts of wolves or dogs as charms. Many consider various parts of a canine to be imbued with magical power, and many spells around the world call for such things. Hunters and warriors from the earliest times wore wolf teeth and fur for fierceness, power, and protection and to take on a "predator" vibe. Vikings were well known for this practice. Wolf skin was not only said to cure rabies, but a wolf tail repelled evil spirits and sleeping with a wolf head under the bed cured bad dreams, though it seems more likely it would cause them!

Dog teeth were said to protect from a variety of problems, including curses, and dog skin was a favorite medium in ancient times for inscribing runes or spells. In one medieval grimoire, it is said that if you wrote the name of a sick person on a dog then drove it off, it also sent the illness away. One wonders what would happen if the dog returned!

Black dogs are often cited as power animals in Western sorcery. Supposedly, blood from such a dog smeared in someone's house breaks all curses in that place, while some of that same blood on your eyelids gave you the second sight. Dog hair was used for protection and was burned in incense to invoke spirits. Such hair is still carried as a charm against evil in several countries.

The charm, power, and aid our canine familiars give us is far more magical than any part of their body, on this we can agree.

But all the different ways dogs were used in ancient sorcery also demonstrates how magical they are.

Dogs have also been used for omens and fortunetelling. While we were in Cambodia, we had a fortuneteller use his dog to pick us a paper inscribed with a fortune. The experience was amazing and really fun, the dog looked at us and then seemed to carefully pick a paper packet that had our day's fortune. Luckily, it was a good one.

Dogs traditionally provide omens through their movements and barking. In ancient Rome, India, and other countries, the barking of dogs helped foretell the future for "augers" or fortunetellers. This is called ololygmancy.

Many oracles we use today are connected with dogs, information we found surprising while researching. The I Ching oracle references dogs in several hexagrams, often as a symbol of positive action and loyalty. There are several runes that reference dogs also.

Dogs feature prominently in the symbolism of three major tarot cards. The first card with the symbolism is the Fool, whose dog barks and pulls at his heels, even as the Fool is about to walk off a cliff. This symbolizes the guarding and guiding aspect of dogs, a symbol of our guardian spirit guiding and protecting us. Dogs (or wolves) are also featured on the Moon trump. Here we see the "gate of the moon" leading to the realm of dream, of psychic work, and to the afterlife. This is an ancient image of the goddess Moon and her guardian dogs. Another tarot card where dogs appear is the Ten of Pentacles. Here the meaning is loyalty, fidelity, the protection of home, and the manifestation of great spiritual accomplishments. This can foretell future wealth and a calm, well-protected home where the presence of a dog indicates prosperity and devotion to family.

It is important to note that canines often had significance when appearing in dreams. Even through the Christian era, this has continued. The Dominican order adopted white and black dogs and these colors as their sacred colors after a dream. Modern dream books describe the appearance of dogs as symbols representing trustworthy, loyal friends or coworkers surrounding and helping you; as happy domestic situations; or as a guiding power to set you in the right direction.

In tea or coffee ground readings, if a dog image appears at the bottom, it means you have a base of loyalty and you can build on this. If in the middle, it means that you can accomplish much due to the loyalty of others. If at the rim, it means you are about to succeed with the help of those loyal to you.

Like you, dear reader, we consider our dog our magical familiar. When we are meditating, doing spellwork, reading the cards, or doing visualization work, our psychic dog is always nearby. We often laugh about the fact that if magic is afoot then so is the dog. Dogs are natural psychics and magical assistants and should be brought into the circle when doing such work.

They bring focus, energy, and dedication in addition to psychic protection. In the spiritual world, canines are considered sacred beings that are useful in magic and psychic work. Many who know this are learning and using dog magic in their own spiritual work in many different cultures. Hopefully, that will include you, dear reader.

Spells, Meditations & Charms

What Type of Mythic Dog Spirit Are You? Meditation

Every dog has his day and every person has an inner canine. How can human beings spend forty thousand years coexisting with canines and not acquire a spiritual dog persona? This meditation is to discover your "dog energy" and, of course, the visions you have will be quite personal. The goal is to relate to your dog "inner canine to inner canine," discovering within yourself your own inner dog and what that tells you about your own self. This may also help you connect with your animal totem, which is your canine guardian and helper spirit.

First, research the types of canines that evolved from the first canine. The key species of canine to choose from are: ancient hound, coyote, dingo, fox, jackal, raccoon dog, and wolf.

You will need:

+ The first rock you see at twilight
+ A stick
+ Some fresh thyme
+ A crystal
+ A small mirror

Go to a natural place with your dog. It could be a park, a hiking trail, or a wooded place of any kind, maybe even your backyard. It should be someplace where other animals (even just squirrels) exist. Do this at twilight, there should be enough light to see but it should be fading. When you see the first rock near your dog's paw pick it up.

Take a stick and walk around in a circle marking the ground with the stick. To summon the elements, say to each direction while offering a bit of thyme:

In the east:

I howl the blowing winds of the eastern gate.

In the south:

I howl the solar fire of the southern gate.

In the west:

I howl the clear water of the western gate.

In the north:

I howl the strength of earth of the northern gate.

Sit down quietly in the circle with your dog. Close your eyes, breathe deeply, and open up your senses to nature and all the natural sounds, smells, and sensations around you. Take some thyme, inhale it deeply, rub a little on your third eye, on your rock, and on your crystal. Now say:

I see with the crystal vision
The power of the earth, water, air, and fire
Birthed by the will of humanity
As the animal that I desire.
I conjure here and now
By the power of breezes, rivers, mountains, and rays,
Now what I become through nights and days
The spirit of the mystic dog reveals.
I see the truth
Of who I am.

Close your eyes and in your mind regress, regress, regress your thoughts. With each breath you become more and more animal, less and less human. You are becoming a primal canine, following your nature. When you feel you are truly being a canine, put the small mirror in front of your eyes and slowly open them. You see before you, yourself, but you are morphed into a canine.

Are you a wolf? A dingo? A fox? Note the color of your fur, notice your expanded senses. Growl hello to your human self, now say:

> O Spirit (kind of canine) *thou art me.*
> *I am thee.*
> *Open my mind*
> *I am now free.*
> *Thank you for this wisdom.*
> *So mote it be.*

When done, close your eyes, rub a bit of thyme on your third eye, and sprinkle it about yourself. With every breath, return to being human. The fur is gone, your eyes become human, and so on.

When done, sprinkle the rest of the thyme on the earth and put the rock back exactly where you found it. The crystal is your own special accessible gateway to your totem animal. You can use this crystal to connect with that spirit anytime. Thank the spirit of that canine power, ask it to teach and empower you, and then go.

Doing Divination for Your Dog Charm

Did you know you could get your dog to tell your fortune? Dogs possess psychic abilities; they can see ghosts, spirits, and even faeries. They are also natural fortunetellers. My grandmother taught me how to tell fortunes with playing cards, I even wrote a book about it titled *Fortune Telling with Playing Cards*. When younger, I practiced telling fortunes to my dog, but I realized it was a little one sided that only my dog got her fortune told. But I wondered, what if my dog could tell me my fortune? Over time I developed a means to have my dog tell my fortune, and now you can use this same divination system to have your dog tell your fortune.

You will need:
+ A deck of playing cards
+ A purple candle
+ Matches
+ Three sheets of purple paper (one for each question)
+ A purple pen
+ Some dried lavender

Shuffle the deck until all the cards are very well mixed. As you shuffle, think of the questions you want answered. Light the candle and write one question per sheet of purple paper. Shuffle the deck three times and give it to your dog to smell.

Lay out all of the cards, facedown in a half circle around your sitting dog. Read the first question aloud to your dog. Call to your dog to choose (or whatever command works for you). Note what card your dog steps on and turn it over; this is your fortune.

The numbers on playing cards relate to the strength of the wish and how close you are before the wish comes to pass. Aces are wild and face cards represent people. It is the same for each of the suits.

Suit of diamonds: Is a yes, especially for anything relating with money.

Suit of clubs: Is a maybe, unless it is a personal goal then it is a conditional yes. It is a goal that will take work.

Suit of hearts: Is a yes, especially if it has to do with love.

Suit of spades: Is a no, unless it has something to do with a problem you must solve, then the answer is yes, with effort.

Here is the explanation for how your wish will happen:

Ace: When you least expect your wish to happen, it does.

Two: The start of something new.

Three: An idea that you have will be noticed.

Four: Somewhere close to home your wish will happen.

Five: Creativity is the only solution.

Six: Make sure that whatever you asked goes slowly.

Seven: This wish involves another person.

Eight: A mysterious way changes your wish.

Nine: Your secret wish will soon be revealed.

Ten: The completion of your wish.

King: A man will have the answer to your wish.

Queen: A woman will have the answer to your wish.

Jack: A young person will have the answer to your wish.

Joker: Your wish takes an unexpected turn.

Keep going if you have more questions (remember your limit per session is three). When done, give your dog seer a treat.

Magical Canine Power Spell

Your dog is a magical animal, but you already know that don't you? The powerful energy that dogs give you and their devotion to any task you ask of them is something to admire. When I was writing this book, I had a dream where the Greek goddess Artemis appeared. Artemis is the goddess of the hunt, whose animals are hunting hounds that lead and guide her through the woods. Artemis appeared and told me, in dreams night after night, that I needed to write this spell down for her because she is a true keeper of canine power and to receive this power she must be invoked. Being a goddess worshipper, I am going to, of course, honor her by doing what she told me to do. So from the goddess Artemis here is her invocation for giving you magical canine power.

You will need:

+ A picture of the goddess Artemis
+ A yellow or golden apple
+ Some pine branches
+ Some white cord

Do this spell outside in the woods when the moon is a waxing crescent. Take the picture of Artemis and lay the apple and pine branches on it. Now circle around the picture and say loudly:

> *I am Artemis! Wild huntress of the silver moon!*
> *I am every canine wild one.*
> *I am satyr, the dog soul.*
> *I am nymph, the Dog Spirit.*
> *Now make of me a powerful*
> *Canine magical soul spirit.*

Now stop circling the picture of Artemis. Pick up the apple, take a bite of it, and now throw the apple into the woods saying:

> *Io Evoe, Artemis!**
> *Io Evoe, Agrotera!**
> *Io Evoe, Pheraia!**

Pick up the image of Artemis and wrap it around one sturdy, wand-like pine branch. Tie it to the branch with the white cord.

Now you have a magical wand you can use anytime you wish to unleash your canine goddess power.

> * *Translation (Latin): Io Evoe, Artemis = Yea! Hail Artemis!; Agrotera = Hail the Huntress!; Pheraia = Hail Lady of Beasts (one of several of her names)!*

Spell to Help Your Dog Find Their Spirit

Dogs, like people, take time evolving their personalities and revealing their inner nature. If your dog needs a bit of a boost to its focus, help centering, or a bit of help finding its inner spiritual power (and don't we all?) then this spell will help your dog access its "guardian spirit" and become a calmer, more emotionally, physically, and spiritually centered dog.

You will need:
+ A special crystal you use for magic
+ Some lemon balm (or rosemary), dried
+ A small dish or shell to burn the herb
+ A branch from your favorite tree

Runes to know:
ᛉ Algiz
ᛝ "Wolf Eye"

Sit in a comfortable place with your beloved dog where nothing will disturb you both. Begin by meditating on your guardian spirit, your inner light always guiding you. Silently ask it to help you in this work.

When ready, with your dog at the center, use the crystal to trace the Algiz rune in the air to north, east, south, and west, then once over your dog. As you do so, say "*Algiz*," and visualize them glowing with white, purifying light.

Light the herb, saying:

> *By Odin, Frey, Freya, and the wolf spirit*
> *Seidr,* bring the light.*
> *By Geki and Freki and the divine wolf spirit*
> *Seidr, bring the light.*
> *By the runes, the Norns,* the nine worlds*
> *Seidr, bring the light.*

Wave the smoke about your dog, blessing your dog. Take the branch of the tree and brush your and your dog's aura, saying:

> *Come through the trees*
> *Wearing your many masks.*
> *The dance of the wolves*
> *Opening the way*
> *Between twilight and sunrise,*
> *Between darkest night*
> *And brightest day.*

With the crystal, trace the Wolf Eye rune on the forehead of your dog—see it glowing in red. At this time, whisper to your dog a spontaneous prayer invoking its spirit to empower, protect, guide, and illuminate your dog. Sit and trance out with your dog, honoring its true spirit. When done, say:

ALUUUUUUU.*

* Translation (Norse): Seidr = magic; Norns = Three Fates; Aluuu = Trance vibration in Seidr.

Telling Your Dog's Fortune

Dogs possess a certain special innate magic about them inviting divination. Dogs were a component of divination rituals for thousands of years. Scrying is the magical act of divination by seeing into the past, learning more about the present, or divining the future. This is often accomplished using a black mirror or a bowl of water. Using scrying as a form of divination is a fun way to tell your dog's fortune. All you need is your dog's water bowl.

Fill up your dog's water bowl and let it drink from it. Have your dog sit on one side of the bowl and sit yourself directly across from your dog. Turn out the lights in your room and make sure it is very dark. You may light one candle in the background if you need more light. Now say:

Thunder, lightning,
Sun, moon, and fire,

Wind and rain,
Ocean's desire,
Cleanse and clean.
Sweep away
Filth and error
All night and day.
*Omnia uno est.**

Now hold your dog's paw over the water bowl and say

By Hekate's deep well,
By the pool of Garm and Lupa,
Let us see what we can see.
Help me, familiar,
Our fortune to see.
*Hierosgamos.**

Now, stare into the water bowl. You should soon start to notice the water in the bowl going in and out of focus as you keep staring into it. Get closer and closer to the bowl, slowly lowering your face until you are just about an inch away from the water. Always keep an arm around your dog.

Now close your eyes and say out loud in a commending voice:

I wish to see (your dog's name)*'s fortune.*

Now open your eyes and again stare into the bowl. An image or series of images should appear before your eyes. That is your dog's fortune. Make sure you talk to your dog about it. When done, say:

The moon gate closed.
The well is clear.
Thanks to the shadows,
Let all disappear.
Uno est nihil.*

Throw the water outside onto the ground, wash the bowl, and give your dog fresh water.

* Translation (Latin): Omnia uno est = All is one;
(Greek) Hierosgamos = The Divine Marriage; (Latin):
Uno est nihil = One is none.

Your Dog & Your Spirit Together Meditation

To truly be in sync with your dog, you need to communicate and work together on an instinctual and primal level, spirit to spirit. We all know that dogs sense our thoughts and feelings, and you are capable of doing this for your dog as well. This meditation will bring you both closer in mind and spirit.

You will need:
+ Calm, peaceful music that your dog likes, or you can do this outside with "natural" sounds
+ A quiet, calm place to be with your dog

Sit across from your dog and just relax as close as possible. Breathe in for the count of ten, hold your breath and count to ten, and breathe out for the count of ten. If counting to ten is too long, then any other amount of time will suffice. Just make sure it is always for the same amount of time for the length of each breath.

As you breathe out each time silently, say:

You are mine.
I am yours.

When you are both calm, listen to the heartbeat of your dog; feel it in your body.

Now notice the breathing pattern of your dog. Try to breathe as closely to that pattern as possible. Feel your spirit expand and flow into your dog with every breath.

Feel your dog's spirit flow into you, with all the alien dog thoughts and feelings. Embrace this, merge with it; become one living being, one breath, and one heart. Now say:

We are that,
We are all.

With all we rise,
With all we fall.

Life and death,
Night and day,
Pain and pleasure,
Ever-changing play.
In the center of all
Is great release.
We are the center of all,
We are peace.

Om Mani Padme Hum* (repeat three times)

Now meditate in this way. Listen with your heart. If you feel a need for an internal mantra to help the process, silently repeat over and over:

Tat tvan asi*

When you are finished, lean your forehead against your dog's forehead, third eye to third eye, love your dog and accept love from your dog. Go out and play.

* Translation (Sanskrit): Om Mani Padme Hum = The Jewel in the Center of the Lotus; Tat tvan asi = You are that.

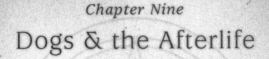

Chapter Nine

Dogs & the Afterlife

Letting Go of a Beloved Dog
& Dog Spirit as Psychopomp,
or Guide of the Dead

Unfortunately, as we finished the rough draft for this book our beloved dog, Thor, who we have been talking about, passed away at the venerable age of seventeen. We are grateful for his long life but also, sadly, prepared for his transition. Nothing can really prepare a devoted dog owner for this letting go, but in our research and discussions we have found comfort in the fact that since the beginning of history, dogs have been associated with the positive aspects of passing on, even to helping us humans make the transition to the "other side." These things comfort us and, we hope, will comfort you as well.

Dogs & Death

Dogs have always been connected with death. Even today it is quite common to see wild dogs roaming smoking "smashan" or human cremation grounds in India and Nepal. We saw this firsthand. Early dogs likely feasted upon corpses, and still do today. Long ago, dogs were seen unearthing buried bones as humanity was developing its funerary practices, and this created an impression. The sight of roaming dogs in the aftermath of battlefields has always been a common one. These ancient associations likely gave us myths of dog gods or spirits of death and as underworld guides and protectors of people in transition.

In Celtic myths, a sacred dog guarded the moon gate leading to the afterlife. The dog's name was Dormarth or "Death's Door." This is almost exactly the same myth described in Hindu tales, where the lunar goddess Sarama is mistress of the death dogs guarding the moon portal to death's realm. Maybe this is the origin of the Moon tarot trump.

We all know the Greek myth of Cerberus, the monstrous three-headed dog belonging to Hades, that guarded the gates to the underworld. Like all dogs, Cerberus can be charmed, and Orpheus used his lyre to sing the dog to sleep when rescuing his beloved Eurydice from the underworld.

Less well known is that Cerberus may be an aspect of the goddess Hecate, who is sometimes shown as dog-headed, thus connecting with the three dogs she is often shown with. Being the ancient mistress of the cosmic crossroads, she is both protector and guardian of the path to the underworld. It was Hecate who led the goddess Demeter to find her daughter Persephone locked away in Hades. Some tarot decks show Hekate on the Moon trump card as well.

The Norse also tell of a giant dog guardian of the underworld called Garm (or Garmr). He guards Helheim. Hel, the Norse queen goddess of the underworld, was said to give birth to "Hell Dogs," which carried souls to paradise. The leader of this death dog pack is a fearsome beast named Managarm, or "moon dog."

There are many dog spirits in the Celtic world that seemingly pass between our world and the next. The Cu Sith, giant green faerie wolf dogs, are an omen or magical warning (sometimes of death) if seen or encountered in the deep wilds of Ireland. In the same part of the world exist legends of the infamous giant black Dog Spirit, whose appearance is always a harbinger of dark tidings. We personally attest to the widespread belief in the big black Dog Spirit because we have seen that almost every town in England has a Black Dog Pub.

Dog "death" spirits appear frightening, but they seem to mythically exist to help us deal with crossing over. Dogs and dog spirits have been guiding human souls carefully into the other world since the dawn of time, according to many faiths.

In the Zoroastrian religion, even today among modern Parsee worshippers, dogs are sacred and help people pass over.

This is a personal story and we hesitate to share it, but it is so germane to this part of the book that we feel we must. After our dog's passing, while performing a funerary ceremony and installing his ashes in a special place in our yard, we were shocked to discover that a young man we were very close to who lived nearby had also suddenly passed away. As we chanted for peace for this young man's transition, both of us received the same vision, which we later shared much to our shock. It was this: our dog, who loved the neighbor boy very much, was guiding the boy's spirit to the afterlife. Due to this young man's sudden and traumatic death, he was a confused soul. We both saw this young man and our Thor leaving this world together. While we previously felt Thor's presence after his passing, suddenly we both knew that he was gone. He waited for our ceremony and then accomplished his final duty, to help guide this young man's soul over to the other side. At least, this is our belief.

We mention this story because as we began doing research on this book, we discovered that this is exactly what dogs and dog spirits are said to do, going back thousands of years, across many very different cultures.

In ancient Greece, the god Hermes, and in Roman myth, Mercury, sent dogs as psychopomps (spirit guides) to assist the spirits of the dead to enter the afterlife safely. Even his caduceus wand could calm Cerberus into letting him and the souls he escorted pass by.

In Egypt, it was the dog-headed Anubis or Anpu ("opener of the way") who did the same. In Japanese, Inuit, and Siberian magic, it is dogs or dog spirits that help a soul find its way through the chaos of the otherworld to paradise or rebirth. The Ainu living in Northern Japan believe the mazelike path through the underworld is filled with helper dog spirits holding torches, waiting to help people make it safely through. Dogs also were said to guide the soul of the deceased to the afterlife in Aztec and Mayan cultures. The Aztec dog-headed god Xolotl sent dog spirits to guide the deceased to the "nine-fold river," through the "jaws of earth" to safety in the blessed afterlife. Even today Parsee worshippers see dogs as guides for and communicators with the dead.

In many ancient cultures, dogs were buried with their owners to help lead them to the otherworld. We know this tradition continues because we have family members buried with the ashes of their beloved dog. In many places, dogs were sacrificed to perform this task, buried with their beloved humans to guide them in the next realm. In Egyptian, Mayan, and Etruscan tombs, where dogs were found buried with people, images of this last journey are depicted with the dog spirit guiding.

Dog gods or spirits also guard the dead, as they did in ancient Egypt, Greece, and Rome. Dogs are honored in many places for doing so. Divine dogs and dog charms magically protect the living from angry ghosts and other evil spirits as they do in China and Japan. Yet mostly dog spirits protect the deceased. In Hindu mythology, it is Sarama the Dog Goddess who guards the gateway between the living and the dead and is said to attend the death god Yama.

Sometimes small images of helper dog spirits are left at a grave to help people pass over peacefully. We ourselves saw dog charms used in Japan during Obon (the festival to honor the dead), and we also saw small clay dog "spirit helpers" put on graves in Oaxaca during the Day of the Dead. In Guatemala, four guardian dogs are often still left on graves to protect the deceased.

Our dogs protect, comfort, and help guide us during our lives. Many cultures have held the belief that they do the same after we pass on to another world. That is true devotion. It is our greatest hope that when we pass on, our beloved Thor will be waiting for us, tail wagging, ready to help lead us to the Summerland.

Spells, Meditations & Charms

Dog Help in Passing Charm

Losing a beloved family member who happens to be a dog is very difficult; sometimes it is almost more than we can bear. Dog owners know that there is a special bond between a dog and its human, a devotion and dedication unmatched in other pet relationships. This is a charm to help you work through the loss of your dog pal with love.

You will need:
+ A photo of your deceased dog
+ Incense or a candle
+ A lock of your deceased dog's hair or something small worn or loved by your dog

+ A small bead or piece of rose quartz that fits in a locket
+ A sprig of fresh rosemary
+ A plate to hold the items above
+ A small generic locket you can wear on a chain or cord

On the night of a new moon, sit with a photo of your deceased dog friend, maybe burn some incense or light a candle. Think fondly of your loved one; feel your loss. Place the items before you on a clean plate. Shed a few tears of sorrow, then place some of your tears on the fur, rose quartz, and rosemary, saying:

> *By the tears of the great dark sea,*
> *Spirit of* (deceased dog's name) *come to me*
> *With joy and love and comfort.*
> *So may it be.*

Place all the items in the locket, saying:

> *By sun of life, moon of death, and fire of love,*
> *By the light from the spirit above,*
> (deceased dog's name) *may you be free.*
> *But may our bond of love and comfort*
> *Bring us both joy and peace for eternity.*
> *By the lady of night of sweet Hekate,*
> *So may it be.*

Place the charm around your neck, say:

Pain and sorrow
Fade away.
In peace and love
We both shall stay.
So may it be.

Wear this charm whenever you wish to feel the eternal soul connection you and your dog will always have. Know that your beloved loyal dog awaits you on the other side. Know that love is eternal and therefore you may let go of the pain but never the memory.

Dog Guiding a Soul Meditation

Dogs are our loyal guides and guardians in life and they can continue to be so in death, or so many cultures and belief systems tell us. This meditation is helping a human friend or relative attain a successful transition to the other side by offering them the help of a guardian guide dog spirit. This dog spirit guide may be the spirit of a beloved deceased dog that has preceded its owner or it may simply be the divine in the form of dog spirit that acts as psychopomp (guide of the dead). This should be done soon after your human loved one has passed and should be done at their grave or at a place where their presence is felt.

You will need:

+ A small container of salt
+ Materials to make a small handmade dog image (from one to three inches tall). It can be made of clay, sticks, paper, or palm leaf. It need not be ornate or fancy.
+ A pen or other writing tool, red ink is best

Sit before the grave of your loved one or in a place where they feel present. You should be alone and have the materials before you. Sprinkle a pinch of salt about you while seeing a purifying light surrounding you. Close your eyes, breathe slowly and deeply, and relax. Let all thoughts flow through you until the image of the departed loved one naturally appears in your mind.

Hold this image and address it with love and compassion. Let your loved one know that if they need assistance, your love will help guide them in the form of dog spirit to the bliss awaiting. Ask if this is okay, the vision will let you know if it is. If so, open your eyes and carefully make the small dog image. While doing so, chant the simple word *Iao*. This great word of power means both "light" and "to heal." Singing it, chanting it, or whispering it are all wonderful ways to enter the right trance.

As you create the dog spirit image, see the light of spirit filling it, see the mission you have assigned it fill it, see your love and will fill it with the goal of guiding the deceased. If you can call forth the energy of the spirit dog, add the name of this dog to your chant. See this spirit dog energy infusing the image and bringing it to life.

When done, write the word *Iao* on the small dog figurine. Breathe on it three times, saying each time:

Iao. By the light of love, help guide (name of deceased) *to spirit.*

Place the figurine on the grave of the deceased, facing north.

Meditate in silence, seeing the dog spirit running up with joy to the deceased and guiding them along a path of light to the other side.

Sit in meditation, open your heart, breathe deeply, and relax. When done, place your hands on your heart and say *Iao* again, filling yourself with love and healing as well.

Sprinkle a bit of salt around you and leave when you will.

Spirit Dog Spell: Working with Your Deceased Pal

If you have a strong magical relationship with your dog or if your dog was your familiar, then death cannot end that relationship. Your magical partner can still aid you and, being a dog, will want to continue to help, guard, and guide you even though they are now of spirit. Dogs, it is said in many traditions, can cross back and forth through the liminal world between life and death, and your familiar can be of great help to you in your spiritual work as a helping spirit if you enter into this relationship with love, respect, and equality. This is not dark magic or necromancy. This is part of an on-going magical relationship entered into with love and trust.

For this spell, you will need a small shrine or a sacred space dedicated to your deceased dog friend. If you plan on working with your dog's spirit, it is likely you already set up a simple altar with items your dog loved, a small photo, and so on. If not, see the Honoring Your Deceased Familiar Charm later in this section.

You will need:

+ Some salt
+ Myrrh incense, in any form
+ A black candle
+ Matches
+ A black mirror or a black ceramic bowl with some water in it
+ Love offerings to your dog; a treat, fresh water, or whatever you like

Begin by tossing a bit of salt to the four directions and tasting a bit, saying:

Out, out, throughout and about,
All good come in; all evil stay out.

Sit in silence for a time. In your mind's eye, see your dog, feel its presence, feel the closeness and love you share. Light the black candle, saying:

By the Queens of Night and Sea,
Hekate, Sarama, Hel, and Belit-ili,
By the gate and way of death,
By faithful Dormarth, Chinvat, and Naraka's breath,
By death dogs Garm, Cerberus, and Calu,
You are with me and I am with you.
Come now forth and work with me.
As I give you love, now let me see.
I with you, you with me.

Wave the black mirror or small black bowl with water carefully over the flame and incense smoke three times saying each time:

Epistston!*

Now, scry (stare deeply with the sight) into the black mirror or bowl. Whisper the name of your beloved dog three times, projecting love and need. At this point, thank your beloved familiar, offer love and blessings, end the spell, and repeat the simple salt banishing.

If your dog's image appears, then you may work with them. Begin by greeting, honoring, loving, and thanking your dog spirit for help and contact. Then ask what you will. Maybe you would like help with divination, finding something, or protection. Once you are in contact, this relation may be built upon. When you are done with the work you need to do, say goodbye to the spirit of your loved one by saying:

Thank you, Queens of Night and Sea,
Hekate, Sarama, Hel, and Belit-ili.
I close the gate and way of death
By Dormarth, Chinvat, and Naraka's breath.
Thanks to death dogs Garm, Cerberus, and Calu.
You are gone from me and I depart from you.
Go now forth and with joy be free,
As I give you love, remember me.

Do the simple salt clearing you began with and blow out the candle. Leave the black mirror or brown water (after pouring out the water on the earth) at your dog's shrine. You now have a deep relationship with your spirit dog, as many shamans have before you.

* *Translation (Greek): Epistston = Cry to urge on a dog.*

Easing Your Dog's Passing Charm

Few things are harder than losing your canine best friend. If your loyal dog passes suddenly, this spell can help the soul of your loved one pass on to the next realm. If you have to facilitate the passing, a hard thing to do, it is best to perform this spell just after the time of passing.

You will need:
+ "Dark" incense of some kind or even a spray scent, if natural
+ A single white candle

- Matches
- A cup of pure water
- A dog bone or favorite treat of your dog
- A small token of your beloved dog: Something worn by your dog or a lock of hair
- Everything should be on a small white plate or cloth

This is to be done as soon as possible after the dog has passed or it can be done if the dog is passing at home just as they pass. Have tissues handy and a glass of pure water for yourself. You should be clean and wear clean clothes, white if possible.

When ready, breathe deeply and rhythmically until you are calm. Visualize light about you and (if present) your dog's body. If your dog is not present, visualize them with you.

Chant *om* three times. Light the candle. See the vibration and the light banish all fear, sorrow, and negativity. Light the incense, saying:

Great mother of the gate of death,
I invoke you by these and all your many names
Artemis, Inanna, Hekate.
Be kind, be helpful, bring peace,
Great opener of the way of death.
I invoke you by these and all your many names
Anubis, Hermes, Yama.
Be kind, be helpful, bring peace.

Open the gates of the unseen.
Guide the soul of this great being to rest.
Open the way, light the way,
This I pray.

Wave some incense smoke about, saying:

By the breath of spirit.

Wave your hand over the candle, saying:

By the light of the divine.

Pour out a little water and say:

May (dog's name) never thirst.

Touch the treat:

May (dog's name) never hunger.

Take up the token and say:

May my love forever embrace (dog's name)
And this love surround me.
So may it be.

Open your arms and, with eyes closed, release your loving dog's spirit—see them follow the path of light to the gate of light and pass on to the other side. You may want to say special words of encouragement, love, and parting. When done, say:

By the light of peace,
Through the light of peace,
I extend the light of peace
With focused will and great love.
Om.

When finished, spend some time breathing until you feel peace.

Let the candle and incense burn out, pour the water out onto the earth, and bury the treat. Know that love is eternal and you and your dog will always share a special bond, no matter what. It is recommended that you keep the token of your beloved pet in a special or sacred place, maybe with a photo of him or her. In this way you can continue to send love and peace as your dog transitions to spirit. Peace.

Letting Go of a Dog Who Has Passed Meditation

Sometimes the grief we feel for a dog that has passed is so deep and persistent it affects our lives in a serious manner. If such grief causes depression or a withdrawal from life, it is a problem and not something our dog would ever want us to endure. This meditation will help you accept the loss of your dear dog friend and, though you will always remember them, allow you to move on with your life.

Go to a place where you often walked your dog. The spot you choose should be in a park, in the woods, or on a hiking trail, someplace with trees and grass and a place to sit. If this location is by a body of water, that is even better. Sit in this place and feel the familiar grief and sorrow of your loss flow through you.

Close your eyes. Before you is your beloved dog, sitting, smiling at you, maybe wagging its tail. It is fine to cry at this point as well. When you are calmed down, eyes still closed, do some rhythmic breathing. Breathe in for three seconds, hold your breath for three seconds, breathe out for three seconds, hold for three seconds. Continue in this manner until you are calm and quiet.

In the earth, draw a trefoil:

Say:

> *By the three*
> *Crone, Maiden, Mother,*
> *Our love is eternal*
> *One for the other.*

Now, eyes still closed, visualize your departed dog sitting there, loving you, not wanting to leave you because of your pain. Begin the rhythmic breathing again, and silently chant as you do so:

> *I love you, I love you, I love you.*

Do this for a few minutes. Then, do the same thing, but this time silently say:

I release you, I release you, I release you.

After a time, visualize your dog getting up, smiling goodbye, and scampering off into the wonderful, exciting, sunlit woods to play and explore.

Finally, when they have moved on, do the same deep counting breathing, this time with your eyes open, internally saying:

I will remember you, I will remember you, I will remember you.

End by simply breathing slowly and deeply and leaving when you wish. You may leave behind an old token of your dog, a worn leash or chew toy.

When done, erase the trefoil, but keep it in your mind and heart always. You will always feel loss, but you can now move on. Repeat this meditation as often as you need. Peace.

Honoring Your Deceased Familiar Charm

The charm in this simple rite is actually a shrine or special place to honor your dog and continue to send positive spiritual support, healing love, and energy to your deceased pet. We owe so very much to our dogs, it is only fitting that we continue to honor and support them after they have passed on. Death is a veil, not a door. Love and support can pass through this veil. When a beloved dog passes, they may be confused or in pain or debilitated. As they pass over, the love, support, and spirit we offer can help guide them to the other side and help them find peace and joy and remember us with love.

You will need:

+ Salt
+ A special place outside or in your home. It can be a shelf, a small cabinet, or a box or even a niche in your garden. Some people keep the actual urn of ashes in the shrine, but that is up to you.
+ A framed photo of your beloved dog
+ A small bowl or cup for water and another for dog treats or food
+ A symbol of your faith
+ A token from your dog; some dog hair, the collar, dog tags, or something similar
+ Flowers, incense, and a candle are needed for the initial installation of the shrine; afterward it is up to you
+ Anything else you feel is appropriate

Before you create your shrine, sprinkle a little salt in a circle around the area saying:

> *Avert, Avert, Avert.*
> *Above and below*
> *And all around,*

All that is bad
Sink into the ground!

Thus cleansing the area of all negative vibrations. Then vibrate the sacred vowels power word:

Aeiou (ayyy eeeee iiiii ooooh ewwww)

And so bless the space while visualizing light filling the area.

Create your shrine. It is best to install the shrine just after your beloved dog's passing; in many traditions twilight is the most auspicious time. As you do so, sing a song or hum something you associate with your departed dog, maybe something that they loved. Visualize your dog with you, helping you, and loving you. When you are finished, say:

I call the primal Wolf Spirit,
Ancestor of all dogs,
You who formed the first bond with us
To witness and bless this shrine.
I call forth the eternal bond of loyalty,
Love, light, laughter, and life
Between man and dog:
By my love and the love of (name of dog)
*Ab initio canem.**
*Amor est vitae essentia.**

Light the candle and incense, and pray silently from your heart to your beloved dog. Then say:

> *This candle is the first and eternal fire that protects you.*
> *This incense is the spirit and power of love that enfolds you.*
> *This water is the love and blood that we share.*
> *This food is the sustenance and support I give you.*
> *These tokens of love and faith*
> *Reflect the love and faith I have in you,*
> *(Name of deceased dog). Here is your shelter.*
> *Here is your place at my hearth.*
> *Here is the place between the worlds*
> *Where I can continue to feed you,*
> *Protect you,*
> *Love you, and pray for you.*

Next, pray to god, goddess, or holy person of your choosing—if you have no preference, simply chant *om* to represent the divine spirit. When done, say:

> *A caelo usque ad terra**
> *A caelo usque ad terra*
> *A caelo usque ad terra*
> *Fiat lux.**

DOGS AND THE AFTERLIFE

The shrine is now consecrated and is a sacred charm for you to use to give love and energy to your departed dog. It is a place to remember and feel its presence when you need it.

Memoratus in aeternum.*

* Translation (Latin): Ab initio canem = From the very first dog; Amor est vitae essentia = Love is the essence of life; A caelo usque ad terra = From heaven centered on the earth; Fiat lux = Let there (always) be light; Memoratus in aeternum = Remembered forever.

Chapter Ten

Dog Stars

Dog Star Magic
& Astrology for
You & Your Dog

One of our favorite times for dog walking is in the evening when the sunset fills the sky and the stars come out over our tree-filled neighborhood. It is relaxing and we all enjoy these meditative walks. Often in winter we watch the brightest stars coming out and none are brighter than Sirius. We usually make a lame joke about how the constellations Canis Major and Canis Minor are the big and little dogs that Orion has to take for a walk just like we take our dog. In a sense this is kind of true, and there is more doggy star wisdom in the heavens than you might think.

Celestial Dogs

Sirius is by far the most famous Dog Star. It is almost universally associated with dogs and has many names all over the world. Sirius is called Sothis in Greek, Sopdet in Egyptian, and T'ien K'uan (or T'ien kou) in Chinese. Sirius resides in Canis Major, the "big dog," and is near to Canis Minor, the "little dog." Both of these Dog Stars are said to have been the pets of various gods and goddesses. Most commonly, the "big dog" is known as Laelaps, the hunting dog of the nearby constellation of the giant Orion. This is reflected in an Arabic name *Al Kalb al Jabbar* ("The Dog of the Giant"). The North Star, by the way, was called the "dog's tail" or "kunos oura."

Sirius was sacred to the Egyptians because its rising signaled the beginning of the annual inundation of the Nile. We were lucky to see temples in Egypt dedicated to the goddess Isis and to the rising of Sirius. The images and hieroglyphs filled us with awe. In such temples, Sirius was worshipped, sometimes as a god in and of itself. It is said spells directed to Sirius increase psychic powers. We certainly hoped that it increased ours.

The annual rise of Sirius represented Isis and her ritual search for Osiris as part of the divine cycle of birth, death, and rebirth. This rising period symbolized the passing of Isis and Osiris through the underworld. The rising of the Dog Star was crucial because it signaled the beginning of new crops and renewal. It was also the beginning of the New Year. The Dog Star itself was directly associated with Anubis. In fact, it was often called the "eye of Anubis" in Egyptian. In ancient Greek, Anubis's star was called "the dog eye" or "Canopis."

The Greeks tended to see the Dog Star as problematic because it was believed to send out negative vibes that could leave people *astroboletos*, or "starstruck." Whether this is a bad or a good thing depends on you! The Romans felt that the intense energies of Sirius led to excessive heat waves in the summer and madness among dogs during the dog days of summer. The connection between summer heat and Sirius appears to be the origin of this phrase. I know our shaggy big dog got cranky during the hot dog days along with most other people.

In the last few years, we and other people interested in alternate spirituality became fascinated with the Mayan and Aztec "oracle" symbols that are often connected with the stars and dogs. The glyph of Xolotl, the last sign of the Aztec zodiac, means "no time" or "chaos," and is the dog symbol at the end of the year representing death, resurrection, and rebirth because he accompanies the sun through the underworld to its renewal. It is said people born under this sign are destined to rule, so powerful was its stellar influence.

In the astrological calendar used by Mayans and Aztecs, the tenth day sign (in the interlocking twenty-day calendar) is that of the dog, called Itzcuintli by the Aztecs and Oc by the Mayans. This symbolizes the Dog Spirit that helps souls transition to the underworld and the spirit world's link with the living. This is a good day for honoring the ancestors and for being trustworthy, and a bad day for trusting dishonest people.

In Chinese mythology, the celestial dog T'ien K'uan (Sirius), "Dog of Heaven," was said to have positive (Yang) and negative (Yin) aspects. It was all-powerful in Taoist mythology and sorcery. Sirius is also said to indicate fate depending on how it shows up in the astrological chart of a Chinese family.

Like most families, when ours goes out for Chinese food we end up engrossed in the Chinese astrology placemats. My son and I were both born in a ram year, my husband is a monkey (is he ever), and our dog was actually born in the year of the ox. No wonder he was so stubborn. In the Chinese zodiac, those born in the year of the dog (Gou) are described as loyal, honest, and faithful to those they love. They worry, possess a sharp tongue, and tend to be picky. However, they are said to be well suited for business, politics, or teaching. Looking at what a "Year of the Dog" might entail (the next two occur in 2018 and 2030) gives us a clear idea of what stellar dog energies may offer us. Stability, loyalty, honesty, and steadfastness are some of the descriptors used for a Dog Year. The Chinese regard Dog Years as very lucky, and if a stray dog comes to a house, it symbolizes the arrival of good fortune. It is claimed that poodles, especially black poodles, bring the greatest luck!

In our experience, we know this is true because great luck has come to us since our black standard poodle arrived in our home. Dogs, it is said, have links to the heavens and to the earth. I am quite sure that all dog owners agree with this because, in our world, dogs truly are the stars.

Spells, Meditations & Charms

Sirius Spell of Protection & Prosperity

This spell is to invoke the goddess Isis as the power of the Dog Star Sopdet or Sirius. The goal is protecting your home or another special place with Dog Star energy and bringing prosperity and happiness. The best time to perform this spell is when

Sirius is actually in the sky; this will vary from place to place. Traditionally it was done in late summer, but it is up to you.

You will need:
+ A small plate, star-themed or deep blue if possible
+ Some natural water collected under the stars
+ A lovely white flower
+ Seven stones, agates are traditional but that is up to you
+ Some incense, something Egyptian such as frankincense or lotus if possible
+ A blue candle
+ Matches
+ You may wish to have a small image of Isis

Assemble all of these items on the plate outside in a quiet, natural place near your house. If you are in an apartment, then do this near a window where you can see the stars and, if possible, Sirius. Light the incense and candle and raise both hands saying:

*Ast Un Nefer.** *
Great Mother of all the Gods and Goddesses,
Root of all life and death,
Manifest nature.
Mother of the Dog Star,
Open, O Isis, the magic gate of Sopdet.
Establish the sacred temple between two rivers,
Between the white and black pillars,

Between the ocean of stars and of tears,
Between the inhalation of first breath
And the exhalation of last sigh.
Isis shine down and come forth from the Dog Star.
*Nuk Ast Per Kua.**

Take up the plate and circle the area to be protected (around your home) and end up back in the center, saying:

*Hra then em kher her-a uat.**
Here is the beginning of all life.
The face of the queen of heaven bends down
To kiss the earth with brilliance, with protection,
*With star power. Tua Ast.**
So the power of Sept, the holy seven-pointed star,
Descends now to bless and empower this sacred place.

Sprinkle yourself, your dog, and the stones with water, then gently pick up the candleholder and move the lit candle in a slow circle about you both. After that, do the same with the incense, and say, seven times:

*Heka en Ast.**

Now, walk clockwise around your abode and place the seven stones around your space at as equal a distance apart as possible. Each time, say *Tua Ast*. Then return to where you began, raise your hands to Sirius, and finish the spell by saying:

Great mother Sothis,
Incarnate here as holy earth,
May the great star goddess protect and bless all.
Heka en Ast.

Blow out the candle, let the incense burn out, and pour out the water onto the earth by your front door.

> ** Translations (Egyptian): Ast Un Nefer = Hail Isis,*
> *Goddess; Nuk Ast Per Kua = Great Isis come forth;*
> *Hra then em kher her-a uat = Here now is the beginning*
> *of life; Tua Ast = Honor to Isis; Heka en Ast = Thus this*
> *magic is accomplished.*

Foo Dog Banishing Charm

T'ien K'uan, the celestial dog in Taoist (Chinese), was connected with Sirius along with both positive and negative celestial omens and energies. This spell is to harness the power of the divine dog to protect and bless you and your dog's home with what is called a "fu" or "foo" charm. Keep in mind the protective power of the Foo Dog. Such paper charms are quite powerful in Taoist magic and this is what you will be making.

You will need:
+ A very clean, high-quality piece of white paper, about 3" x 6"
+ A small brush
+ Some red and black ink or watercolors

Your dog should be present and you should do this at night when the stars are out. If Sirius is in the sky it is even better.

Outside, with some light to see what you are doing, hold the paper up to the stars and visualize the radiance of the starlight filling you, your dog, and the paper, saying:

> *By the Three Kings of Heaven,*
> *By the Celestial Star Goddess,*
> *By the Supreme power of the Blessed Goddess Kwan Yin,*
> *I call down the beneficent powers of T'ien K'uan.*
> *Guan Yin Shi Pu Sa.**
> *Guan Yin Shi Pu Sa.*
> *Guan Yin Shi Pu Sa.*

Having previously looked at some pictures of traditional Foo Dogs, do your best to paint a simple version of the celestial dog at the top of the paper in black and a star of seven points under this in red, in the center of the paper. As you do whisper over and over:

> *Om ma ni bei me hom.**

When finished, ask your dog to bless this charm. Then gently take his right paw, paint a bit of the black and red ink or water color on the paw, and make a paw print under the star on the paper, saying:

> *T'ien K'uan empower this Fu.*

Erlang empower this Fu.
Kwan Yin empower this Fu.

Hold it up to the stars (to Sirius if possible) and see it glowing with star power and say:

Om ma ni bei me hom.

The foo charm is now empowered. Wash your dog's paw. The foo charm may be hung up wherever it will best protect from evil or, if you are in great need for immediate results, it can be burned when dry. If you do this, do so outside and chant the above mantra as you burn it.

> * *Translation (Chinese): Guan Yin Shi Pu Sa = Goddess Kwan Yin, we honor and invoke you now; Om ma ni bei me hom = Han Chinese version of the Tibetan Om Mani Padme Hum—The Jewel in the Center of the Lotus.*

Best Dogs for Your Astrology Sign

The best dog spell for you is to find the right dog that matches your spirit, heart, and energy. Here are some suggestions, though your higher self will know when you have found the right dog.

Aries

Active breeds that can keep up with a fiery, energetic Aries are a good choice. Some dogs need more exercise than others and these types of breeds enjoy any kind of activity that includes you both. Many dogs need someone just like an Aries, who also likes to play hard and is sports minded. Dogs that do not enjoy sitting around waiting for its person to get off the couch can get easily bored. If you like keeping busy and perhaps even compete in sports, along with a four-legged friend you will need a dog that will challenge you to live life to the fullest. A daily companion that will push you physically further than you thought possible.

Some of the best breeds for Aries are:

Border collie

Irish setter

Vizsla

Jack Russell terrier

Dalmatian

Great Dane

If you want a breed that will jump at the chance to get the action-packed Aries to push themselves to the limit, then these types of breeds will join you in the fun of an active enjoyable life.

Taurus

Breeds content to hang out and take it slower are the best kind of pet for Taureans. Taking it easy and not being in a rush is a good thing, right? If you like puttering around in gardens, doing projects in your home, or just taking a stroll through your neighborhood, you will need a laid back breed. A dog that prefers to watch you do all the work while it dozes is a great dog for earthbound Taurus. A loyal furry friend that keeps out garden intruders and protects your domain will give you peace of mind, while you happily move from one project to another. Taureans like to eat and cook and they can tend to overeat, so giving their dog people food is something they can't resist.

Some of the best breeds for Taurus are:

Bulldog

American Staffordshire terrier

Bullmastiff

Basset hound

Chinese crested

Cairn terrier

Gemini

Busy, busy Gemini likes to keep on the move and embraces one change after another. A breed that is flexible enough to have its human pull them from one environment to another is a good choice for a Gemini. A Gemini is social and has a wide variety of friends, so a dog that can get along with anyone is a good choice. A Gemini is intelligent and will need a smart dog, too.

A breed that can join in Gemini's ever-changing kaleidoscope world and also has a sense of playful humor that can keep its Gemini entertained is ideal. Breeds capable of matching and adapting to changes while still joining the sign of the twins in their merriment are the best to accompany Gemini.

Some of the best breeds for a Gemini are:

Cardigan Welsh corgi

Poodle

Weimaraner

West Highland white terrier

Labradoddle

Scottish terrier

Cancer

Home-loving, beach-loving Cancers need a dog that both loves the water and enjoys spending time with their person in their "crab hideaway." A human who will throw sticks in the water for them and also welcome them to lie near the hearth is best. Even if you're a Cancerian who does not live near a beach, a water-loving breed will happily jump into any kind of water, be it lakes, rivers, ponds, or pools.

Cancerians will also need a dog that does not object to a bath, to get rid of that dreaded wet dog smell before they enter the snug home of the crab. Cancers are intuitive and sensitive, so a calm breed is a wise choice.

Some of the best breeds for Cancers are:

Schipperke

Labrador retriever

Cocker spaniel
Bolognese
Havanese
Basset hound

Leo

Leos get along with fierce and protective breeds. Breeds that are uncommon attract them—Leos like an out of the ordinary type of pooch. Others coming across this exotic breed will ask, "What kind of dog is that anyway?" Special showy types of breeds that have "manes" to match their person are great. They should also have that regal or elegant air.

Leos like to entertain, so a dog that is good at parties and being around a lot of different people in its home is called for. Lying around doing nothing also appeals to Leos, so a dog that has short spurts of energy and then lies napping next to a Leo's side is an excellent choice.

Some of the best breeds for Leos are:
Cavalier King Charles spaniel
Afghan hound
Chow chow
Bichon frise
Keeshond
Saluki

Virgo

Orderly Virgos need the type of dog that does not shed a lot and leaves their home tidy. Virgos can be fine with the fussy breeds that need coaxing to eat, play, and sleep. Many Virgos prefer organic, healthy food, and will insist that their dog eat likewise. Dogs that are fine with being well groomed, bathed regularly, and having their teeth brushed are good choices. An established schedule that is always followed makes it easier for Virgos to stay on track, and a dog that likes routine is a mandatory match. A dog that is intelligent and can easily be trained to follow rules is absolutely perfect for a Virgo who needs perfection.

Some of the best Virgo breeds are:

Brittany Spaniel

Chihuahua

Basenji

Schnauzer

Wheaten terrier

Pug

Libra

Dogs that won't be hard on the balanced and harmonious homes that Libras create are the best breeds for the sign of the scales. Libras love books and love having a dog that enjoys lying tranquilly while their person has their nose in a book. Libras are peace-loving souls who need peace-loving dogs that do not bark a lot or get into fights with other dogs. Libras need good-natured, sweet dogs that would never cause discord in the home and dogs that are well mannered. Libras need dogs that love cuddling and to give kisses and be petted in return. The right dog gives a Libra an even happier home.

Some of the best Libra breeds are:

Airedale terrier

French bulldog

Boston terrier

Greyhound

English springer spaniel

Maltese

Scorpio

Dogs that are a good match for the scorpion are dogs that are loyal, especially to their one special person. Breeds that are fierce and protective, that prefer one person to answer to, and that always mind their human are what Scorpios need. Scorpions that need to have home or business guarded need to count on dogs that take their job very seriously. Intuitive and intelligent dogs that can match Scorpios' intensity in anything they both put their minds to are best. Big-hearted dogs that are passionate and love to be needed are just right for Scorpios, and sensitive dogs that can pick up on Scorpios' hidden moods are perfect.

Some of the best breeds for Scorpios are:

German shepherd

Boxer

Tibetan Mastiff

Akita

Bloodhound

Shiba Inu

Dingo

Sagittarius

Larger dogs, smaller dogs with big personalities, and those that are outgoing and fun do well with those born under the sign of the archer. A perfect match for a Sagittarius is a dog that is friendly, playful, and has lots of energy. A companion dog that is very social and loves everyone they meet works perfectly for Sagittarians. Sagittarians need dogs that can easily adapt to changes in the environment and that can travel well. Having a dog that is a best friend and can get along with both people and pets makes it all the more fun for the Sagittarius.

Some of the best Sagittarius breeds are:

Australian cattle dog

Golden retriever

Bearded Collie

Yorkshire terrier

Saint Bernard

German shorthaired pointer

Capricorn

Breeds that are dependable, intelligent, and independent are good dogs for Capricorns to consider. Easily trainable dogs that can learn fast and tend well work best with those born under the sign of Capricorn. Dogs that are independent, bright, and that can keep their person company at the office would work for a Capricorn. A breed of dog that enjoys long hikes and other strenuous activities and that are agile enough to keep up with the goat are also smart choices.

Some of the best Capricorn breeds are:

Bernese mountain dog

Old English sheepdog

Norfolk Terrier

Goldendoodle

Xoloitzcuintle

Great Pyrenees

Aquarius

Aquarians like different-looking dogs that make others stop and ask what kind of unusual, special dog is it. Any breed that has a special talent that they shine while doing is what an Aquarian would find the best fit. Some breeds have a better sense of humor than others, and those born under the sign of the water bearer need a dog that makes them laugh. Dogs that stand out and are a little different would do well with an Aquarian.

Some of the best dogs for Aquarius are:
Dachshund
Beagle
Irish wolfhound
Rat terrier
Newfoundland
Rhodesian ridgeback

Pisces

Pisces needs a quiet, restful breed that is gentle in disposition. Dogs that are sweet and kind to everybody they meet are a smart choice. Daydreaming, sitting in the Piscean lap—dogs that like these things are best. Breeds that are content to snuggle while their Pisces dreams away are perfect. Pisceans will need a dog that loves the water as much as they do. Pisces will enjoy breeds that are sensitive and also attractive to look at. Breeds that can go with the flow and are supportive and aware of the shy Piscean are great. A sensitive Pisces needs the total devotion and love of their dog but also they need a calm breed.

Some of the best breeds for Pisces are:
Shih tzu
Papillon
Portuguese water dog
Whippet
Lhasa aposo
Cairn terrier

Dog Days Sothis Charm to Protect Your Dog

Summer is the most active time for you and your dog with hiking, exploring, running about, and so on. During the hottest time of the year, your dog is most susceptible to over-heating, accidents, and too much friskiness. This was the time called the dog days, and ancient Greeks and Romans protected themselves and their pets from becoming *astroboletos*, or "starstruck." The source of this belief, Sirius, could also be invoked to protect from the same phenomena. This charm calls upon the power of Zeus, or Jupiter, whose loyal dog protected him as a child. It is a simple charm to protect your dog, by Jupiter.

You will need:
+ A small charm with a star on it (or use the back of a dog tag)
+ An awl or some other item that can scratch metal
+ Three leaves from your favorite oak tree
+ Bowl of rainwater or spring water

When ready to do the spell, have all the items gathered before you. Tear up one leaf and scatter it about you and your dog, saying:

> *Io Pater,**
> *Protego nos.**
> *Protego nos.*
> *Protego nos.*

Take another leaf and tear it up, put it in the bowl of water, and say:

> *By the tree of the mighty Jove,*
> *By the heavens that are above,*
> *Cooling powers we do bring*
> *Like the rains and winds*
> *By Jupiter and Zeus,*
> *And cooling heavens above,*
> *I protect my dog from the heart*
> *With love.*

Now, take the charm, if you have one, and scratch the astrological symbol for Jupiter ♃ and the words *progego canem** on the back of it. Another possibility is to scratch a simple star and that phrase on the back of a dog tag. As you do this, repeat *Jovis protego nos.*

When done, rub the charm with an oak leaf, fill it with intense Sothis energy, and say:

> *Spiritus ducentia protego canem**
> *Tui gratia Jovis gratia sit protego*
> *Protego canem.*

Sprinkle water around and let your dog drink some.

Gently rub your dog with that third oak leaf from nose to tail, seeing the Sothis light and the protective power of Jupiter cover and protect him. When done, bury the leaf and go have fun in the sun.

    * *Translation (Latin): Io Pater = Great Father (Jupiter); Protego nos = protect us; Spiritus ducentia protego canem = Beautiful divine power protect my dog; Tui gratia Jovis gratia sit protego = We thank you, Jupiter, for your protective power; Progego canem = Protect my dog.*

Orion Spell of Power

Sometimes your dog is low-energy, a bit sad, maybe even not feeling great or just feeling his age. This spell is to give your dog a lift, a bit of power, or maybe some healing energy if it is a bit under the weather.

You will need:
+ Some pure spring water
+ A lodestone or small iron magnet
+ A silver bowl

This is best done during the hot dog days of summer when Sirius is out and dogs are feeling heat issues. Place the lodestone or iron magnet in the bowl of water and leave it out under the stars for one night. Go to a place where the stars are visible, it is best if Orion is in the sky. Visualize a circle of light above you. With the bowl of water in your hands, raise them to Orion and Sirius, saying:

> *By Powerful Orion and Sirius,*
> *Io Evoe.*
> *Bless this elixir of star power.*
> *So mote it be.*

Early the next day collect the bowl of water. When you are ready to empower your dog, take him to a cool, natural place, sprinkle some water on the hot pooch, and say:

> *As I am Orion the giant,*
> *You are Laelaps the hound.*
> *As I am Zeus the powerful,*
> *You are Kyon Khryseos the sun dog.*
> *As I am Hekate the protector,*
> *You are Sirius the glowing.*
> *As you give me love, protection, and power,*
> *So I now give you love, protection, and power.*

Give your dog some of the water to drink (not the lodestone). Then pour it in a circle around your dog, saying:

> *Io Evoe Sothis.**

You may bury the lodestone or use it later on. Have a nice energetic walk.

> ** Translation (Greek): Io Evoe Sothis = Praise to Sothis.*

The Astrology of Your Dog

Some dogs are closer to being true to the characteristics of their breeds than of their astrology sign, although I have found that there is a general connection between astrology and breeds that is worth mentioning here. Still, every dog is different and each has its own personality that may or may not fit the general attitude of the breed. For example, my standard poodle is a Taurus and a great guard dog, even though standard poodles are not known for being fierce or deeply protective of turf. So while general astrological knowledge can help us understand our furry friends, it is not definitive!

Aries

Many Aries dogs are full of energy and spirit and enjoy sports activities. They generally love ball tossing, fetching sticks, and chasing anything that runs, especially other dogs. They can be inquisitive and happy to play games. Many dogs born under the sign of the ram often have a keen ability to work and play hard. An Aries dog may help you get into shape even if it is just with leisurely walks.

Taurus

Many dogs born under the sign of the bull are patient, strong, and very laid-back. Many of these outdoor-loving dogs will wait tirelessly whenever you tell them to stay. Taurus dogs might be content to sit around and watch what you are up to in a very peaceful way. Some can be stubborn, however, so you may have to work hard to train them to do what you want them to do.

Gemini

Lots of dogs born under the sign of the twins are smart, inquisitive, and curious. Many are eager to learn what you ask of them, and these quick-to-learn smarties are said to be the type of dog that you can teach even the hardest trick to. Some can be very active to the point of being hyper and because of their social nature they often play well with other dogs and will encourage dog friends to join in on the fun.

Cancer

Dogs born under the sign of Cancer are said to be sweet and gentle and may love to stay at home in a quiet atmosphere, especially with other members of the family. Many of these dogs like to eat many things and will beg for even the most unusual food. Keeping a variety of doggie treats handy is an important habit for the cancer dog owner. These dogs traditionally enjoy water fun. Those who want a slower pace of life would do well with some Cancerian dogs.

Leo

According to astrology, a Leo dog can be a showy dog and enjoy looking good and showing off its newly groomed coat. Many Leo dogs are loyal, protective, and maybe a bit vain. They may be a little lazy, and they can be in no hurry to get up and move at times. Many Leo dogs like to be petted and fussed over. Leo dogs are said to be good with children and will play with them until the child stops, and they can protect well, too.

Virgo

Traditionally, Virgo dogs are said to be fussy and may turn up their noses at some delicious dishes. It can take time to find what the dog born under the sign of the virgin will like, but simple, healthy, organic dog foods are the best. Some do not adapt well to sudden change, and they can look at you with that "Now what?" face. Some Virgo dogs just like to have everything explained to them in advanced. It is said that Virgo dogs can make excellent therapy dogs.

Libra

A dog born under the sign of Libra may be smart, fair, and like to look good. If you have other pets in the home, many dogs that are born under the sign of the scales will treat them equally, and it is said they like to feel equal to the other pets and people.

Many Libra dogs are able to easily understand the correct way to behave and what is expected.

Scorpio

Scorpio dogs are intense and are said to have traits that can be awesome or iffy depending on the dog, such as being possessive, sexy, or secretive, which some consider connected with Scorpio. They can be great guard dogs that will defend you or your home to the bitter end. These are also very loyal dogs that are at times very possessive about anything they call their own, including you. A Scorpio dog, no matter what size or age, will make sure all is safe. If you want a breeding dog, a Scorpio dog will be happy to do just that. These dogs do not liked to be watched when they are doing something private, like burying a bone. If you want an intense and loving dog that will be protective, loyal, and independent, this is your dog. These great dogs take their job seriously.

Sagittarius

It is said that the traits of the Sag dog include being enthusiastic, playful, and just all around fun. Even if you don't want to play, many Sag dogs will convince you otherwise. Lots of these dogs are adventuresome so you might need to keep an eye out to make sure that they do not stray far or get into mischief. Their wagging tails and constant movement often make them joyful pets, the type that can cheer you up when life has you down.

Capricorn

Many dogs born under the sign of Capricorn are dutiful, intelligent, and great workers. Traditionally, it is said that these dogs strive to please by doing a great job at any task at hand. Many are bright and can be easily trained. They can be the type of dog that will follow directions and stick to the rules and boundaries you ask of them. A Capricorn dog can be a patient dog, willing to wait until you ask something new of them. Some dogs born under the sign of Capricorn are great at jobs and often are more efficient than other dogs.

Aquarius

Many dogs born under this sign are all-around great dogs with many talents and abilities. The Aquarius dog can be full of good humor and often has an inquisitive nature. They sometimes are entertaining and like inclusion in any activity their person wants to do. Some Aquarian dogs like to show off and also might be a little different than the typical dog. Dogs born under this sign can be upbeat, smart, and enjoy the outdoors.

Pisces

Many sensitive, sweet, and gentle dogs are born under the sign of Pisces. Some of these dogs like to be groomed and pampered. They tend to like to be a lap dog, no matter their size, and they will often lie on you until you ask them to get down. Many are kind and sensitive to their best friend's needs (that's you!) and if you need comforting, some Pisces dogs will be happy to do just that.

Dog Chakra Colors & Their Attributes

Did you know your dog has chakras just like you? Chakras are energy centers in the body and each chakra has colors and meanings to them. There are seven chakras and you can activate their qualities by tapping into them at any time with the use of their colors. Dogs see color differently and cannot see some hues, so it is up to you to pick the right color for your dog. Harnessing chakra power is very beneficial for many and you can use this energy to do many things for and with your dog.

Choose colors carefully for your dog's collar, leash, water and food bowl, or other personal possessions. In this way you can unleash chakra energies with colors. Your dog's chakras are like a human's chakras. The seven chakras begin at the base of the spine and end at the crown of the head.

Red Chakra

The first chakra or base chakra promotes stability and security and the feeling of being grounded. Anything red you want to put on your dog's clothing, leash, or collar will help make a hyperactive dog calmer. The red chakra also brings out your dog's possessiveness and territorial tendencies; this is great for when you want your dog to be a super guard dog.

Orange

The second chakra of your dog is orange and is located on the lower abdomen/genitals. This is the perfect color to use in breeding, because the orange chakra controls sex. It will bring a feeling of well-being and pleasure to your dog. Your dog is going to want to play more, but it also brings out your dog's curiosity and friendliness. If you want your dog feeling and acting more like this, then put anything orange on your dog.

Yellow

The third chakra is located on the lower belly and is the color yellow. This chakra is the chakra of happiness and fun, two great qualities in a dog.

If you want a more self-assured dog, confident in any situation, then putting some yellow on your dog will help harness that chakra and bring those qualities out even stronger. Yellow helps make a winning personality and a dog everyone will want to be around; it brings out their inner sunshine.

Green Chakra

The green chakra is the heart center and is the chakra of loyalty and love. It is a good color for dogs needing to learn how to bond, and for people who want to form a stronger bond than they already have. This chakra will also bring out the peaceful nature of your dog and bring out its gentler side. It is also a good color for bringing out the best in them in terms of developing a loving nature with any person or other animal.

Blue Chakra

The blue chakra is located on your dog's throat. It is the chakra that aids communication. If your dog needs help in understanding what you are asking it to do or how to act, try putting something blue on it. This chakra will also make your dog trust more and help it be more engaged with you and the world around it. The blue chakra also helps with giving you both insights into understanding each other's language.

Indigo

This chakra is located at the third eye (center of forehead). It is perfect for developing a psychic bond with your dog and making it more psychic in general. This is a great chakra to bring out in your dog attributes of insight, wisdom, and intelligence. If you want to do any dream work with your dog and connect in dreamtime, put this color on your dog before you both lie down to sleep.

Violet

This chakra is located on the crown of the head. It is a great chakra for giving your dog confidence, devotion, and spiritual energy. It is also the chakra color you need for your dog to tune in to its spirit and also connect with your inner spirit. To make your dog noble, spiritual, and meditative use violet. This is a great chakra for both of you to focus on during meditations together and also the chakra color to use if your dog needs help when going through something stressful.

Magical Dog Stones

Stones are an excellent way to help your dog. They can be used in a variety of ways, from helping heal to bringing calm to your pet. Using stones is a very powerful and easy way to bring the desired energies into the life of your dog and yourself. Stones can help you achieve the desired effects you want. All you need is the stone that offers the energetic qualities you desire for your dog. It is not necessary to buy big or pure stones for better results; it is not price or the size of the stone but the intent behind it. Stones can be placed in dog beds, added to collars, kept on a leash, or used to empower water that is then strained and given to your dog. Think of all the ways these stones can magically help your dog.

Agate: To use for dogs that need to be more grounded and have more energy.

Amber: Calming affect for dogs that are stressed and need a boost of happiness.

Carnelian: To help give dogs more focus and self-control.

Garnet: Use for dogs that need better health and energy.

Jasper: A stone for dogs to activate chakras for healing. Dog chakras begin at the base of the spine and end at the crown of the head.

Kunzite: The angel stone is used to open dog's hearts to become more loving and to connect as a guardian spirit.

Malachite: This stone is used to aid in prosperity energy and to manifest all things good and grounding.

Obsidian: Obsidian is the wizard stone and can aid dogs to become more psychic and see ghosts or work magic.

Petrified wood: Gives dogs the ability to connect with nature and other animals.

Quartz: A stone to transmit to dogs the expectation of desirable behaviors.

Rhodonite: This stone helps dogs reach their full potential in anything they do.

Rose quartz: The stone of love helps dogs to bond and to be friendlier.

Ruby: Protects dogs that are shy and afraid of their own shadow or banish phobias of any kind.

Sapphire: Strengthens the ability to reach any dog goals and to aid in expectations.

Smokey quartz: To balance sexual energies for dogs with a lot of pep.

Topaz: Brings wisdom and intelligence to even the most stubborn dog.

Tourmaline: Helps ease stress in any type of change in a dog's life.

Turquoise: Brings health and healing to dogs that need to feel better.

A Glossary of Dog Spirits & Dog-Loving Gods & Goddesses

Aesculapius: Greek—God of healing whose symbol was a dog

Anubis (Anpu): Egyptian—The jackal-headed god of opening the way of death

Apollo Cunomaglus: Greek/Roman/Celtic—Apollo of the hunting dog in the United Kingdom

Arawn: Celtic—Lord of the underworld (Annwyn, Annwn), a leader of the wild hunt and its dogs

Ares (Mars): Greek—God of war associated with war dogs

Argo: Greek—The loyal dog of the divine hero Odysseus

Artemis: Greek—Moon goddess of the hunt; dogs were her symbol

Arthur: British/Celtic/possibly Roman—Divine hero king, has Cavall, the divine dog

Asteria: Roman star goddess often associated with Sirius

Barong: Mystical Lion Dog of Bali and Balinese legends and rituals

Bau (or Baba): Sumerian/Akkadian—Goddess associated with healing and dogs

Belit-ili: Akkadian—Goddess of healing whose symbol was a dog

Bhairav Shiva: Hindu—Terrible aspect of Shiva whose vehicle is a dog

Black Dog: United Kingdom/Europe—A spook dog spirit who appears to foretell death

Buddha: Trans-Asian—Buddha was guarded by a Lion Dog and loved dogs

Calu: Etruscan—Wolf-lord of the underworld

Canis Major: A very famous constellation (with Canis minor) of Orion's dog; *see* Sirius

Cerberus: Greek/Roman—Three-headed huge dog god who guards the underworld

Cernunnos: Celtic—Horned god of nature and wildlife accompanied by dogs

Chinvat: Philippines—A god whose partner, lightning, is a divine dog

Coyote (Old Man Coyote): There are many tribal variants, like the Aztec Coyolto

Cú Chulainn: Celtic—Famous divine hero associated with dogs and loyalty

Cu Sith: Celtic—Giant green faerie dog with supernatural powers and an omen

Cunomaglus: Celtic/Roman—Minor dog god of hunting found in the United Kingdom

Dattatreya: Hindu—Guru god who was always shown with devoted dogs

Dharma: Hindu—Dharma has many meanings and is used in two distinct ways in this book. In both instances, though it is not translatable, it generally means "right way" or "correct actions." But in pre-Vedic religion (what later became Hinduism), Dharma was a god-form that personified the correct way of doing things (Rta), for example, in line with ritual mores or traditions. In Buddhism, Dharma became a key part of the philosophy generally meaning "Univeral or Cosmic Law" within a Buddhist context.

Diana: Roman—Goddess of the moon, famed for her hunting dogs, similar to Artemis

Dingo Ancestor: Australian Aboriginal—An ancestor spirit and divine helper

Epona: Celtic/Roman—Horse goddess associated with dogs

Erlang: Chinese—God whose divine dog helped defeat the Monkey King and monsters

Faunus: Roman—God, similar to Pan, associated with wolves and the Lupercalia

Fenris: Norse—Giant wolf god who bit off Tyr's arm and brought Ragnorok (the end of the world)

First Dog: The first ancestor of the Sioux and other people, such as Mongolians

Flora & Vina: Roman—Agricultural goddesses (flowers and vines) honored with dogs

Foo Dogs or Fu Dogs: Lucky or magic dogs; *see* Shi

Fox Spirit: Pan-Asian—Trickster spirit who is in many tales and myths; *see* Inari

Fushi: Chinese and Pan-Asian—Luck or Power Dog; *see* Shi

Garm (Garmr): Norse—Underworld dog god, like Cerberus

Geki & Freki: Norse—Wolf spirit companions of Odin

Grim: Old English—A phantom spirit dog or a dog sacrifice at the base of churches

Gula: Sumerian—Goddess of healing whose symbol was a dog

Gwydion: Celtic—Hero who also was said to lead the wild hunt

Hachiko: Japanese—Hero dog, semidivine now, symbol of eternal loyalty

Hades (Pluto): Greek/Roman—God of the underworld, Cerberus's master

Hecate (Hekate): Greek (pre-Greek)—Goddess of magickal crossroads; her helpers are dogs, often three, often black; connected with Cerberus

Hel: Norse—Goddess of the underworld whose symbol was a dog

Hercules Kynagidas: Greek—Hercules the Hunter whose helper was a divine dog

Hermanubis: Egyptian, Greek—Dog-headed god who blended Hermes and Anubis in Ptolemaic Egypt; his worship spread throughout the ancient world

Hermes/Mercury: Greek/Roman—Dog of travelers, thieves, merchants, etc. As the psychopomp or guide of the dead, his symbol was a dog. He can be dog headed.

Herne: Anglo-Saxon—Horned god of the wild, said to lead the wild hunt with his dogs

Holda (Holle): German—Goddess of nature, said to lead the wild hunt with her dogs

Inari: Japanese Shinto—Goddess of rice and prosperity whose spirit/aspect was a fox

Innana: Sumerian—Goddess often associated with the moon and dogs

Inu: "Dog" in Japanese, also "dog kami" or spirit

Isis: Egyptian—Isis is one of the greatest Goddesses of ancient Egypt, though not until the later dynasties by which time she had "absorbed" many other goddesses and their attributes. She is everything from a great Earth Mother to a supreme sorceress who managed to trick Ra out of his powers. Among her many attributes was a connection in spells to dogs and dog magic.

Itzcuintli: Aztec—Dog god of the twentieth day in the Mayan cyclical calendar (Mayan: Oc)

Jupiter (Jove): Roman Zeus—Also associated with a golden dog

Kitsune: Japanese—Fox spirit; *see* Inari

Kwan Yin (Quan Yin, Guan Yin): Chinese—Goddess of compassion and mercy

Kyon Khryseos: Greek—"Golden dog" who guarded the infant Zeus in some myths

Laelaps: Greek—Orion's great hunting dog, also sometimes ascribed to Zeus

Legba, Elegua, and Exu: African/Afro-Caribbean—Gods of the crossroads who have dog helpers

Lupa: Roman—Divine wolf-mother of Romulus and Remus, the divine founders of Rome

Maira: Greek—A minor goddess associated with Sothis or Sirius

Mary: Christian—Mother of Jesus, often shown with a dog, symbol of faith and devotion

Minerva/Athena: Roman/Greek—Dogs were associated with both these goddesses

Ninisinna: Sumerian—Also called Gula, mother of Gilgamesh whose symbol was a dog

Nin-karoc (Nin-Karrak): Another name for the Babylonian goddess Nintinugga, goddess of healing and wife of the god Ninurta. She is the same as the Akkadian goddess Bau who later became Gula, though she was likely originally a separate goddess. All had the dog as their symbol and protector, and dogs were honored at her temple.

Nodens: Celtic—God of deep waters and hunting whose aspect and symbol were a dog

Odin: Norse/Germanic—All-father who has pet wolves and was said to lead the wild hunt

Ogu (Ogun, Gu): African/Afro-Caribbean—Dog of war and strength, associated with dogs

Omisto: Japanese Shinto—God of suicide, associated with dog spirits

Orion: Greek—Giant hunter demigod constellation whose dogs include Canis Major

Osiris: Egyptian—God of the dead who took dog form when he traveled in the underworld

Pan: Greek—Horned god of wild nature, who bred dogs for Artemis; associated with wolves; Pindar called him "the shape-shifting dog of the great Goddess"

Pan Ku: Chinese—Creator god who was said to be a dog and founded humanity

Robigus: Roman—God of grain disease who was propitiated by dog sacrifices

Romulus and Remus: Roman—Divine founders of Rome, raised by Lupus, a wolf

Rudra: Hindu—God, meaning "the howler," conflated with Shiva; his vehicle is a black dog

Rundas: Hittite—Dog god

Saint Christopher: Christian—Saint strongly associated with dogs due to his everlasting devotion and loyalty, sometimes shown as dog-headed

Saint Dominic: Christian—Head of the Dominican order symbolized by an attack dog

Saint Domino: Christian—Saint who heals disease symbolized by a dog

Saint Guinefort: The only dog who became a saint. This saint was actually a greyhound dog belonging to a knight in thirteenth-century Lyon, France. He was mistakenly killed defending the infant son of the knight from a serpent when the knight thought the dog was the aggressor. Buried in a well with trees about, this became a shrine for a "saint" and both are still venerated today, but not recognized by the Catholic Church.

Saint Hubert: Christian—Saint symbolized by a dog

Saint Roch: Christian—Saint symbolized by a dog

Sarama: Hindu—Goddess connected with the moon

Shi: Chinese—"Lion dogs" who are powerful demi-god guards and magic makers

Siegfried: Germanic—One of many divine heroes or tribal founders raised by a wolf

Silvanus: Roman—God of the woods, fields, and boundaries, whose divine helper was a dog

Sirius (Sothis, Sopdet): From several cultures—The important divine Dog Star in many cultures

Skin Walkers: From several cultures—Dog Spirits who can become human

Suijin or Suitengu: Japanese—Shinto Kami who protects and eases childbirth and is symbolized by a dog

T'ien K'uan (or T'ien kou): Chinese—Good and bad divine star god connected with Sirius

Taranis: Celtic/Gaul—God of lightning associated with and could be a dog

Tishub: Hittite—Dog-headed, winged god of lightning

Tu Kueh: Turkish—Mythic hero who prehistorically founded the Turkic peoples, was raised by a "blue" she wolf

Tyr: Norse/Germanic—Hero/war god whose arm was eaten by Fenris, associated with wolves

Wepwawet: Egyptian—War god who was a wolf god (or jackal) and protector of the king

Werewolf: Cross cultural—People who become wolves or part-wolves; *see* skin walkers

Wild Hunt: Celtic/European—The myth of a divinely led spirit hunt with spirit dogs and led by Odin or Herne or Holda; it sweeps through the skies as fall becomes winter

Xolotl: Aztec—Dog-headed god of the underworld who guides the sun to rebirth

Yama: Pan-Asian—God of death who guards the underworld with two four-eyed dogs

Yudhishthira: Hindu—A star of the *Mahabarata* (Hindu epic), his name indicates a great warrior. He was the son of King Pandu and Queen Kunti and became a great and noble king who, through the grace of Indra, outlasted all his brothers and ascended to heaven, but not without his dog. It was revealed then that his loyal dog was really the god Dharma. The moral, it seems, being that "dharma always follows you even after death."

Zeus/Jupiter: Greek/Roman—Father God who has a divine dog and used divine war dogs

Zoroaster: Parsee—Divine founder of Zoroastrianism (now Parsee) whose holy book *The Avesta* praises dogs and has an entire section on caring for dogs, the spiritual power of dogs, etc.

Bibliography

A-to-Z Photo Dictionary of Japanese Buddhist Statuary. "*Shi-Shi Lions.*" Accessed July 16, 2015. http://www.onmark productions.com/html/shishi.shtml.

A-to-Z Photo Dictionary of Japanese Buddhist Statuary. "*Suijin.*" Accessed July 16, 2015. http://www.onmark productions.com/html/suijin.html.

Adkins, Lesley, and Roy Adkins. *Dictionary of Roman Religion*. New York: Facts on File, 1993.

Ananda Saraswathi, Yogi. "Dogs in the Hindu Way of Life." *Anandashram.* January 30, 2014. https://anandashramblogg .wordpress.com/2014/01/30/dogs-in-the-hindu-way-of-life/.

Andrew. "Mystery & Lore of the Black Dogs from Hell!" *Paranormal Encounters.* October 26, 2014. http://www.para normal-encounters.com/wp/mystery-lore-black-dogs-hell/.

Andrews, Tamra. *A Dictionary of Nature Myths*. Oxford, UK: Oxford University Press, 1998.

Andrews, Ted. *Animal-Speak*. St. Paul, MN: Llewellyn Publications, 1993.

Atsma, Aaron J., ed. "Seirios." *Theoi Greek Mythology*. Accessed July 23, 2015. http://www.theoi.com/Titan /AsterSeirios.html.

Biedermann, Hans. *Dictionary of Symbolism*. New York: Meridian Book, 1992.

Brewer, E. C. *Dictionary of Phrase & Fable*. Hertfordshire, UK: Wordsworth Editions, 2001.

Burns, Cathy. *Masonic and Occult Symbols Illustrated*. Mt. Carmel, PA: Sharing Press, 1998.

Carrasco, David. "Canines." *Mesoamerican Cultures*. Accessed July 16, 2015. http://media.smith.edu/media/ereserves /pdf_files/hillyer/misc_docs/canines.pdf.

Cavendish, Richard. *Mythology: An Illustrated Encyclopedia*. New York: Rizzoli International, 1980.

Chevalier, Jean. *The Penguin Dictionary of Symbols*. London: Penguin Books, 1994.

China Highlights. "Year of the Dog." Accessed July 23, 2015. http://www.chinahighlights.com/travelguide/chinese -zodiac/dog.asp.

Christie, Anthony. *Chinese Mythology*. London: Hamlyn Publishing, 1975.

Clark, Rosemary. *The Sacred Tradition in Ancient Egypt*. St. Paul, MN: Llewellyn Publications, 2000.

Cooper, J. C. *Dictionary of Symbolic & Mythological Animals*. London: Aquarian Press, 1992.

_____ . *An Illustrated Encyclopaedia of Traditional Symbols*. New York: Thames and Hudson, 1987.

Coren, Stanley. "The Truth about Cats and Dogs—by the Numbers." *Psychology Today*. May 14, 2013. https://www .psychologytoday.com/blog/canine-corner/201305/the -truth-about-cats-and-dogs-the-numbers.

Crystallinks.com. "Chinese Creation Myths." Accessed July 22, 2015. http://www.crystalinks.com/chinacreation.html.

Dainow, Amanda. "The Mythology and Healing Powers of Dogs." *Singing Nettles Herbal Clinic*. June 7, 2011. http://singingnettles.blogspot.com/2011/06/mythology -and-healing-powers-of-dogs.html.

Dog Breed Info Center. "How to Say 'Dog' in Different Languages." Accessed July 2, 2015. http://www.dogbreedinfo.com /languages.htm.

Dream Therapy Now. "Dog Dreams." Accessed July 21, 2015. http://www.dreamtherapynow.com/id30.html.

Drury, Nevill. *Dictionary of Mysticism and the Occult*. San Francisco: Harper and Row, 1985.

Encyclopædia Britannica. "Diana (Roman religion)." Accessed July 23, 2015. http://www.britannica.com/EBchecked /topic/161524/Diana.

Faculty.gvsu.gov. "Sumerian Myth." Accessed July 16, 2015. http://faculty.gvsu.edu/websterm/sumerianmyth.htm.

Fogle, Bruce. *The Encyclopedia of the Dog.* New York: Dorling Kindersley, 1995.

Fries, Jan. *Cauldron of the Gods: A Manual of Celtic Magick.* Oxford, UK: Mandrake of Oxford, 2003.

_____ . *Helrunar: A Manual of Rune Magick.* Oxford, UK: Mandrake of Oxford, 1993.

Gill, Sam D., and Irene F. Sullivan. "About Coyote." *Modern American Poetry.* Accessed July 16, 2015. http://www.english.illinois.edu/maps/poets/g_l/louis/coyote.htm.

Gordon, Stuart. *The Encyclopedia of Myths & Legends.* London: Headline Books, 1993.

Gosford, Bob. "Dingoes and Dogs in Indigenous Culture." *The Northern Myth.* May 29, 2014. http://blogs.crikey.com.au/northern/2014/05/29/dingoes-and-dogs-in-indigenous-culture/.

Grimassi, Raven. *Encyclopedia of Wicca & Witchcraft.* St. Paul, MN: Llewellyn Publications, 2003.

Guirand, Felix, and Richard Aldington. *New Larousse Encyclopedia of Mythology.* London: Hamlyn Publishing Group, 1973.

Hausman, Gerald. *The Mythology of Dogs*. New York: St. Martins Press, 1997.

Houston, Jean. *Mystical Dogs: Animals as Guides to Our Inner Life*. San Francisco: New World Library, 2004.

Indaus. "Yudisthira at Heavens Gate." January 28, 2005. http://indaus.blogspot.com/2005/02/yudisthira-at -heaven-gate.html.

James, Jenny. "The Dog Tribe." Accessed July 22, 2015. http://www.southernanthro.org/downloads/publications /SA-archives/2006-james.pdf.

Jamshedji Modi, Jivanji. "The Funeral Ceremonies of the Parsees." *Zoroastrian Archives*. Accessed July 16, 2015. http://www.avesta.org/ritual/funeral.htm.

Johnson, Buffie. *Lady of the Beasts: The Goddess and Her Sacred Animals*. Rochester, VT: Inner Traditions, 1994.

Jones, Alison. *Larousse Dictionary of World Folklore*. New York: Larousse, 1996.

Jones, Prudence, and Pennick, Nigel. *A History of Pagan Europe*. London: Routledge, 1995.

Khandro Net. "Dog." Accessed July 22, 2015. http://www .khandro.net/animal_dog.htm.

Leach, Maria. *Funk & Wagnalls Standard Dictionary of Folklore, Mythology, and Legend.* San Francisco: HarperCollins, 1972.

Lindemans, Micha F. "Kimat." *Encyclopedia Mythica.* Last modified August 25, 1999. http://www.pantheon.org/articles/k/kimat.html.

Liungman, Carl. *Dictionary of Symbols.* New York: W. W. Norton, 1991.

Lurker, Manfred. *A Dictionary of Gods and Goddesses, Devils and Demons.* London: Routledge & Kegan Paul, 1987.

MacCana, Proinsias. *Celtic Mythology.* London: Hamlyn, 1970.

Manansala, Paul Kekai. "The Dog Story: Dog as Deity, Ancestor and Royal Animal." Accessed July 21, 2015. http://asiapacificuniverse.com/pkm/dogstory.htm.

Mark, Joshua J. "Dogs in the Ancient World." *Ancient History Encyclopedia.* June 21, 2014. http://www.ancient.eu/article/184/.

Matthews, Boris, trans. *The Herder Symbol Dictionary.* Wilmette, IL: Chiron Publications, 1991.

Matthews, John, and Caitlin Matthews. *The Element Encyclopedia of Magical Creatures.* New York: Sterling Publishing, 2005.

Messick, J. "Canines in Greek and Roman Mythology." *Booksie*. May 28, 2010. http://www.booksie.com/non-fiction/essay /jmessick/canines-in-greek-and-roman-mythology.

Michael, Linda. "'Black Dog': The History of an Expression." *Blackdoginstitute.org*. Accessed July 23, 2015. http://www .blackdoginstitute.org.au/docs/Michael.pdf.

Monkhbayar, Ch. *Mongolian 108 Wonders*. Ulan Batar, Mongolia: N. Batjargal, 2014.

Moonlight (aka Amanda). "Superstitions of the Wolf." *Werewolves.com*. Accessed July 16, 2015. http://www.werewolves .com/superstitions-of-the-wolf/.

Myths Encyclopedia. "Animals in Mythology." Accessed July 23, 2015. http://www.mythencyclopedia.com/Am-Ar /Animals-in-Mythology.html.

Native Languages of the Americas. "Native American Dog Mythology." Accessed July 23, 2015. http://www.native -languages.org/legends-dogs.htm.

Noodén, Lars. "Animal Symbolism in Celtic Mythology." *University of Michigan*. Updated November 1992. http://www -personal.umich.edu/~lars/rel375.html.

Nozedar, Adele. *The Illustrated Signs & Symbols Sourcebook*. London: HarperCollins, 1989.

Papa Legba. "The Kingdom of This World." Accessed July 16, 2015. https://www.msu.edu/~williss2/carpentier/part2/legba.html.

Pickering, David. *Cassell Dictionary of Superstitions*. London: Cassell, 1995.

Rose, Carol. *Spirits, Fairies, Leprechauns, and Goblins: An Encyclopedia*. London: W. W. Norton, 1996.

Sakson, Sharon. *Paws & Effect: The Healing Power of Dogs*. Los Angeles: Alyson Books, 2007.

Sargent, Denny. *Dancing with Spirits: The Festivals & Folklore of Japan*. Stafford, UK: Megalithica Press, 2010.

Schostak, Sherene. *Dog Stars: Astrology for Dog Lovers*. New York: Viking Studio, 2006.

Sfrc.ufl.edu. "The Pact of Fire: A Lakota Sioux Legend." Accessed July 16, 2015. http://sfrc.ufl.edu/plt/activities_files/The_Pact_of_the_Fire.pdf.

Sheppard Software. "Dog of Greek Mythology." Accessed July 16, 2015. http://www.sheppardsoftware.com/content/animals/animals/breeds/dogtopics/dog_mythology.htm.

Simpson, Jaqueline. *A Dictionary of English Folklore*. Oxford, UK: Oxford University Press, 1998.

Sionnach, Laurel. "Dogs in Mythology & Folklore." *Hemlock and Hawthorn*. February 17, 2013. https://hemlockand hawthorn.wordpress.com/2013/02/17/dogs-in-mythology/.

Sophia. *Fortune in a Coffee Cup*. St. Paul, MN: Llewellyn Worldwide, 1999.

Stuckey, Johanna. "'Going to the Dogs': Healing Goddesses of Mesopotamia." *MatriFocus* Web Magazine for Goddess Women. Accessed November 3, 2014. http://www.matri focus.com/IMB06/spotlight.htm.

Sun Signs. "Chinese Dog Horoscope 2014." Accessed July 22, 2015. http://www.sunsigns.org/dog-horoscope-2014/.

Symbol Dictionary. "Celtic Animal Symbols: Hound, Wolf, Dog." Accessed July 15, 2015. http://symboldictionary .net/?p=936.

Szczepanski, Kallie. "History of Bali's Calonarong Dance." About Education. Accessed July 23, 2015. http://asian history.about.com/od/indonesia/ss/barongdance.htm.

Telesco, Patricia. *Dog Spirit: Hounds, Howlings, and Hocus-Pocus*. Rochester, VT: Destiny Books, 2000.

Trubshaw, Bob. "Black Dogs: Guardians of the Corpse Ways." *At the Edge*. Updated November 2008. http://www.indigo group.co.uk/edge/bdogs.htm.

Turner, Patricia. *Dictionary of Ancient Deities*. Oxford, UK: Oxford University Press, 2000.

Valliant, Melissa. "Dog Saliva Has Healing Powers, Fact or Myth?" *HellaWella.com*. April 27, 2014. http://www .hellawella.com/fact-or-myth-dog-saliva-has-healing -powers/21004.

Venefica, Avia. "Dog Symbolism in Tarot." *Tarot Teachings.com*. Accessed July 16, 2015. http://www.tarotteachings.com /dog-symbolism-in-tarot.html.

Walker, Barbara. *The Woman's Dictionary of Symbols & Sacred Objects*. San Francisco: HarperSanFrancisco, 1988.

_____ . *The Woman's Encyclopedia of Myths and Secrets*. San Francisco: HarperSanFrancisco, 1983.

Walker, Benjamin. *The Encyclopedia of the Occult the Esoteric and the Supernatural*. New York: Stein and Day, 1977.

Weir, Anthony. "A Holy Dog and a Dog-Headed Saint." *Dissident Websites*. Accessed July 16, 2015. http://www.beyond -the-pale.co.uk/dogsaints.htm.

Worth, Valerie. *A Crone's Book of Magical Words*. St. Paul, MN: Llewellyn Worldwide, 2002.

Yu, Anthony C., trans. *The Journey to the West, Revised Edition*. Chicago: University of Chicago Press, 2013.

To Write to the Authors

If you wish to contact the authors or would like more information about this book, please write to the authors in care of Llewellyn Worldwide Ltd. and we will forward your request. Both the authors and publisher appreciate hearing from you and learning of your enjoyment of this book and how it has helped you. Llewellyn Worldwide Ltd. cannot guarantee that every letter written to the authors can be answered, but all will be forwarded. Please write to:

Sophia and Denny Sargent
⁒ Llewellyn Worldwide
2143 Wooddale Drive
Woodbury, MN 55125-2989

Please enclose a self-addressed stamped envelope for reply,
or $1.00 to cover costs. If outside the U.S.A., enclose
an international postal reply coupon.

Many of Llewellyn's authors have websites with additional information and resources. For more information, please visit our website at http://www.llewellyn.com.